Embracing and Educating the Autistic Child

Embracing and Educating the Autistic Child

Valuing Those Who Color Outside the Lines

Nicholas D. Young
Kristen Bonanno-Sotiropoulos
Melissa A. Mumby

Foreword by John Elder Robison

ROWMAN & LITTLEFIELD
Lanham • Boulder • New York • London

Published by Rowman & Littlefield
An imprint of The Rowman & Littlefield Publishing Group, Inc.
4501 Forbes Boulevard, Suite 200, Lanham, Maryland 20706
www.rowman.com

Unit A, Whitacre Mews, 26-34 Stannary Street, London SE11 4AB

Copyright © 2019 by Nicholas D. Young, Kristen Bonanno-Sotiropoulos, and Melissa A. Mumby

A note on the cover: The heart is filled with the colored puzzle pieces known to represent autism. The picture of the hands connecting symbolizes the love, value, and support from those who are dedicated to working with this population.

All rights reserved. No part of this book may be reproduced in any form or by any electronic or mechanical means, including information storage and retrieval systems, without written permission from the publisher, except by a reviewer who may quote passages in a review.

British Library Cataloguing in Publication Information Available

Library of Congress Cataloging-in-Publication Data

Names: Young, Nicholas D., 1967– author. | Bonanno-Sotiropoulos, Kristen, author. | Mumby, Melissa A., 1977– author.
Title: Embracing and educating the autistic child : valuing those who color outside the lines / Nicholas D. Young, Kristen Bonanno-Sotiropoulos, Melissa A. Mumby.
Description: Lanham, Maryland : Rowman & Littlefield, [2019] | Includes bibliographical references.
Identifiers: LCCN 2018031027 (print) | LCCN 2018043459 (ebook) | ISBN 9781475846904 (electronic) | ISBN 9781475846881 (cloth : alk. paper) | ISBN 9781475846898 (pbk. : alk. paper)
Subjects: LCSH: Autistic children—Education. | Children with autism spectrum disorders—Education.
Classification: LCC LC4717.5 (ebook) | LCC LC4717.5 .Y68 2019 (print) | DDC 371.94—dc23
LC record available at https://lccn.loc.gov/2018031027

∞ ™ The paper used in this publication meets the minimum requirements of American National Standard for Information Sciences Permanence of Paper for Printed Library Materials, ANSI/NISO Z39.48-1992.

Printed in the United States of America

To my good friend, Peter Bittel. Peter is a highly accomplished entrepreneur who has dedicated his life to advocating for individuals with disabilities. On a personal level, Peter has been a trusted confidante and even better friend, especially during my more challenging life periods. May he know I am grateful for his sympathetic ear; while appreciating that I view him as a valued mentor. He should be proud of this life of service he has and continues to lead.—N. D. Y.

To my dear friend Sean Kane. Throughout the years you have encouraged me to soar by being my cheerleader, even when I have been down, you were always there bringing the light to show me that I was strong. I will always remember the millions of beads we have wasted!—K. B. S.

To my mother, Linda, who always taught me to believe in myself. Thank you for never giving up on me even when times were tough. I hope I've made you proud.—M. A. M.

Contents

Foreword ix

Preface xiii

Acknowledgments xvii

1 Understanding the Autistic Mind: Characteristics of Autism 1
2 Protecting and Serving Autistic Individuals: Understanding State and Federal Policies 9
3 Creating the Foundation for Success in Students with Autism: From Assessment to Educational Goals 19
4 Developing Effective Educational Programs for Autistic Students: Challenges and Solutions 31
5 Helping Students with Autism Find Success in the Classroom: Promising Interventions 45
6 Applied Behavior Analysis and Effective Classroom Instruction: Strategies that Foster the Best in our Students 57
7 Developing Social Skills: Social Interactions and Social Awareness 69
8 Effective Collaboration with Related Service Providers: The Importance of Teamwork 81
9 Working with Families of Autistic Students: Understanding and Coping with the Stressors 91
10 Transition Planning for Autistic Students: Preparing for Postsecondary and Workforce Transitions 101

References 119

About the Authors 131

Foreword

The landscape for autism support in primary and secondary schools is quickly changing. It begins with how autism is perceived: from disability to difference. We have seen a shift from mediating learning disabilities to accommodating and supporting learning differences. Therapies have evolved and language to describe autism has changed, with this shift being just one manifestation. Twenty years ago our perception of autism was limited to describing the ways in which a student might be disabled. Today we recognize that autism confers a mix of disability and exceptionality, and teachers are encouraged to find and nurture exceptional traits.

Prior to the DSM-5 revision, autism was divided into classic autism, PDD-NOS, and Asperger syndrome. Kids diagnosed with classic autism generally had significant language impairment. A large percentage had intellectual disabilities. PDD-NOS kids were more mildly impaired and might be seen as more eccentric than disabled; they often had severe executive function challenges. Asperger kids were generally bright, with good language skills but with a significant social disability.

Schools developed packages of services that were associated with each diagnostic label. Those services had been assembled following the 1990s release of DSM-4, where PDD-NOS and Asperger were presented to educators for the first time. Since 2015, everything is consolidated under the overarching heading of Autism Spectrum Disorder (ASD). While that may be more correct in light of emerging knowledge, it upsets the systems that schools have put in place these past two decades.

Today's educators and therapists will deploy those same services, and newly developed services, but their allocation will be based on a variety of "severity indices" that are adjuncts to the ASD diagnosis. Tomorrow's student may be described as having ASD with mild or severe language impairment, where before students might have been labeled with autism as opposed to Asperger.

While students may ultimately receive similar services as compared to years past, it is more confusing. One diagnostic label—ASD—now characterizes a range of students from intellectually disabled to genius, and from nonspeaking to exceptionally articulate.

Autism experts are also discovering a wide range of medical conditions that accompany autism. The realization that school children may suffer from previously unrecognized anxiety, intestinal pain, seizures, and a host of other conditions places a new level of responsibility on school clinicians. Even the brightest and seemingly least-disabled students are at risk for these complications.

Professionals are learning about issues like this from actual autistic people. In the past services were developed and delivered by nonautistic clinicians and researchers. While those people surely had the best interests of students at heart, they were unable to truly understand autistic thoughts and experiences. The one person who inherently understands those things is another autistic. Openly autistic adults were rare a generation ago but the surge of child diagnoses in the 1990s has yielded a significant pool of diagnosed adults, some of whom have advanced training in special education and therapy.

As more and more autistic adults appear, it is inevitable that local and national leaders will emerge in educational, medical, and social advocacy. Those leaders will probably become more vocal with respect to special education policies and autistic children. The application of techniques like applied behavior analysis (ABA) will be questioned to a greater degree. Autistic leaders will call for new therapies to be developed, and for changes to old ones.

A decade from now autism specialists in schools may find themselves answering to autistic adults in several areas. Autistic adults are likely to seek positions of responsibility overseeing state and local special education policy, employment policy, and special education itself. Openly autistic people are also entering higher education in greater numbers, and educators are certain to find themselves working alongside autistic staff in the schools of tomorrow.

When students and nonautistic staff see openly autistic people in the workplace, their view of autistic students must necessarily evolve. If adults are openly autistic and embrace that identity, the old ideas of "curing autism" and "normalizing behaviors" will not seem very viable.

The neurodiversity paradigm is likely to take root in public schools, just as it is in universities today. *Neurodiversity* is the idea that a certain amount of neurological variation is a natural part of human diversity. The idea that autism, attention-deficit/hyperactivity disorder, dyslexia, and other inborn differences are selected by evolution provides a new perspective on what were once seen as defects.

What is disabling in an American public school may be lifesaving in another context. By embracing the idea of neurodiversity we recognize that truth. Evidence of that has been before us all along, but it went unrecognized until now. Every trait of autism has the potential to confer disability and exceptionality. For example, an autistic student who is stuck studying and talking about one topic of interest is disabled when that prevents doing schoolwork on a range of topics. Later when the child is an adult and has learned some moderation, that time, drive, and focus can make the autistic adult into a top expert.

Scientists have observed that typical children look at faces, while autistic children prefer geometric shapes. Studies like that—while making valid observations—carry inherent value judgments as to which observation is "correct." If a person's goal is successful social engagements, the preference for faces confers a clear advantage. A person whose focus is the machines will have an advantage with the autistic gaze.

School is a very social environment: one where autistic people tend to be at a disadvantage. A kid who is disabled in that context might later become a star as a network engineer or machine operator, even as more social peers are effectively disabled among the machinery and technology. The neurodiversity paradigm recognizes that dichotomy and places it in a context of larger evolutionary purpose. It helps to understand how much disability is a social construct. In the network engineer's world, a social gadfly would be the one who was disabled. Many aspects of autism are like that—in the proper place our differences are just that, differences. Autism presents other challenges that would be disabling in almost any context. A person who could not speak would be disabled in more places, likewise a person with a cognitive disability would be disabled almost everywhere also.

The neurodiversity perspective says that some amount of neurological variation is part of the typical human range, where at the extremes neurological difference shades into pathology. Autistic people with more extreme communication challenges might be farther into the pathological range, even as their differences occur naturally.

The fact that differences are a natural part of us does not deny the reality of disability. The job of tomorrow's educators is to respect the range of human diversity and support each student in order to achieve the best quality of life possible. Part of that is getting through school: something that was and remains a great challenge for kids with social disability, whatever their other gifts.

This book, *Embracing and Educating the Autistic Child: Valuing Those Who Color Outside the Lines*, has come at a critical point in education. With the continued rise in the diagnosis of autism for school-aged students—

particularly in the United States, but very applicable around the world—the need for educators to be well-informed in understanding and working with this population is a necessity. The authors have conducted an extensive review of the current literature as well as seminal pieces discussing best practices when working with autistic students. Within the pages of this book, the reader will find essential information pertaining to the unique characteristics of the autistic student, promising evidence-based practices beyond just academics, effective components of programming planning, and the importance of transition supports and services, to name a few.

—John Elder Robison

John Elder Robison is a best-selling author, educational consultant, public speaker, autism advocate, and an autistic adult. John is well known for his various books on autism including Look Me in the Eye, Raising Cubby, Switched On, *and* Be Different. *He holds various prestigious positions on many governmental agencies advocating for the rights of autistic individuals. These positions include subcommittee chair of the Interagency Autism Coordinating Committee within the U.S. Department of Health and Human Services, member of the Steering Committee for the Autism ICF Core Sets Project for the World Health Organization, review board member of the U.S. Department of Defense Autism Research Programs, and committee cochair for the Institute for Autism Research. John also holds such positions as Neurodiversity Scholar in Residence at the College of William and Mary in Williamsburg, Virginia, and visiting professor for the School of Education, Human and Health Sciences at Bay Path University in Longmeadow, Massachusetts.*

Preface

Embracing and Educating the Autistic Child: Valuing Those Who Color Outside the Lines is an informative and timely book for educators, administrators, related service providers, community partners, and family members working or living with an individual diagnosed with autism. This book is armed with the most current research in the field of educating autistic students. The unique academic and emotional challenges present in an autism spectrum disorder (ASD) diagnosis require that educators and parents become skilled and knowledgeable in the most effective strategies and interventions for addressing the distinct academic, behavioral, and social demands that accompany it.

Currently, ASD affects one in fifty-nine individuals within the United States and accounts for 1% of the world population (Centers for Disease Control and Prevention, 2018b). Autism is considered a spectrum disorder, appearing in early childhood, with deficits commonly occurring in communication and language, social interactions, behavior, and sensory stimulation (Luiselli et al., 2008; Webber & Scheuermann, 2008; Zager, Wehmeyer, & Simpson, 2012).

Students with ASD may require a wide array of supports, from minimal to substantial, in order to achieve academic and social success within the learning environment. Current literature suggests that not all teachers understand the implications of teaching a student with ASD and further, many educators are not adequately trained in working with this population of students (Zager, Wehmeyer, & Simpson, 2012). As a result, it is important for educators to develop a solid foundation for understanding the characteristics of ASD and their impact on learning, behavioral needs, and social development; thus, the need for a book such as this is critical for the field of special education.

In addition to the aforementioned reasons, our motivation for writing this book stems from several concerns:

- *the knowledge that autism is the fourth largest disability category served under the Individuals with Disabilities Education Improvement Act;*
- *the belief that learning environments that are well-structured and educationally rich are essential to the success of autistic students;*
- *the commitment to ensuring that all students with autism can experience positive academic, emotional, behavioral, social, and independent gains;* and
- *the confidence that partnering with families, practitioners, educators, and peers best supports all students, including those with autism, in the quest for improved outcomes across all domains.*

Each chapter provides the reader with extensive knowledge surrounding all facets of working with ASD students. Within chapter 1, the reader will gain a deeper understanding of the plethora of symptoms associated with an autism diagnosis. Further, individuals will become familiar with the statistics, prevalence, and ongoing research in the field of autism, in order to increase awareness.

Chapter 2 considers both state and federal policies for individuals with ASD. Examination of various agencies and their agendas are highlighted as a means of increasing awareness and providing the reader with options for further avenues of resources.

The many methods for diagnosing autism are the focus in chapter 3. The chapter includes in-depth examinations of current assessment tools and their requirements. Also provided is information on how an autism diagnosis affects learning and what can be done to overcome these challenges. The reader is provided with strategies for increasing not only academic skills, but communication skills as well.

Effective programming for students with ASD as well as the challenges to appropriate programming are discussed within chapter 4. Challenges such as teaching and assessment factors are examined as well as free and appropriate public education and writing appropriate individualized education programs. In response to these challenges, we provide reasonable and simple suggestions for overcoming these encounters as well as an exploration of appropriate classroom and assessment accommodations and modifications.

Research-based practices are extensively discussed within the pages of chapter 5. We highlight the necessary components to planning effective educational programming for autistic students and delve into the most promising evidence-based practices, interventions, and strategies for increasing academic, social, and behavioral outcomes for this population of students.

Chapter 6 explores the theory and principles of applied behavior analysis (ABA) as well as other promising treatments for autistic students. ABA is a strategy backed by over fifty years of research and theory and is an evidence-based instructional strategy that supports behavior change and has been proven to produce desired outcomes for individuals with autism (Webber & Scheuermann, 2008). The reader will also become familiar with other promising approaches such as discrete trial teaching, naturalistic teaching, and pivotal response training.

Chapter 7 dives into the development of social skills and social awareness as well as supporting social interactions for students with autism. We begin with an examination of how deficits in social awareness contribute to difficulties in social interactions experienced by many autistic individuals. Appropriate and beneficial approaches for increasing social awareness are investigated and considered within the pages as well.

Collaboration and support are at the heart of chapter 8. This chapter looks at the benefits of continued partnerships and cooperative relationships with related service providers such as Board Certified Behavior Analysts (BCBAs), speech therapists, occupational therapists, and community partners. The reader will gain extensive knowledge surrounding how to successfully engage in these collaborative efforts to benefit the needs of the autistic student.

Chapter 9 highlights the difficulties and struggles that a family of an autistic student may experience. The chapter offers insight into the stresses and impacts on the household unit, including siblings, spouses, and extended family. Provided are strategies and resources available to support and assist individuals through the journey.

Our final chapter examines the critical need for successful and targeted transition planning, supports, and services for autistic individuals. From the development of self-advocacy skills to postsecondary supports, this chapter highlights best practices across the grade spans in relation to ensuring successful transitions. Also discussed are the federal mandates between K–12 and postsecondary institutions, the critical skills required to ensure positive lifelong outcomes including self-advocacy, self-determination, and independence skills as well as goal setting.

In totality, the chapters offer a comprehensive examination and an enhanced understanding of the unique and wonderful qualities and needs of the ASD student as well as how to plan and implement effective programming in order to achieve positive educational, social, and behavioral outcomes for this population.

This book was written by a team of seasoned education professionals who combined have over forty years of experience in the field of special education. At various times during our careers, one or more members of our team of authors has been a special education teacher and/or administrator, a clinical psychologist, a counselor, and/or a university education professor who taught graduate courses focused on disabilities. It is our combined unwavering compassion and dedication to the field of special education in general—and autism in particular—that drove us to write a tome that acknowledges and supports an awareness for this unique and endearing population of individuals.

Our goal in writing this book was to help educators and families understand the best practices associated with an ASD diagnosis. It became, however, our hope that all who read it will gain a renewed appreciation for the gifts and personal triumphs of students with autism and their families. More than inviting our readers to digest the content alone in the pages to follow, we also encourage those who can to join us in assuming a greater advocacy role on behalf of individuals with ASD across their lifespan.

Acknowledgments

It has been said that individuals are blessed if they are surrounded by a few special friends and colleagues who enrich their lives. For us, Sue Clark has been such a person. While she made a noteworthy contribution to this book as its chief editor and cheerleader, she also continues to distinguish herself as a treasured friend. Our heartfelt thanks go to Sue for being a tireless member of our writing team and a never-ending source of optimism and kindness.

Chapter One

Understanding the Autistic Mind

Characteristics of Autism

Although autism is a fairly new disorder, its characteristics can be traced back over 200 years; yet within the last decade, the prevalence of autism has increased over 100% making it the fastest growing developmental disorder (Centers for Disease Control and Prevention, 2018a). Autism is considered a spectrum disorder; however, there are certain characteristics that commonly occur within all individuals diagnosed. Deficits in communication and language, social interactions, behavior, and sensory stimulation are common (Luiselli et al., 2008; Webber & Scheuermann, 2008). Currently, autism affects 1 in 59 individuals within the United States and accounts for 1% of the world population (Centers for Disease Control and Prevention, 2018b).

There has been extensive research into the causes of autism, yet no definitive origin has been determined. Research has identified atypical brain function, structures, and shapes within autistic individuals (Centers for Disease Control and Prevention, 2018e). At this time, there are no medical tests to determine the prevalence of autism; thus, it is critical that if autism is suspected, interventions are started immediately (U.S. Department of Health and Human Services, 2018). The diagnosis of autism relies on the use of observational data gathered from extensive surveillances relative to communication, social interactions, and behaviors (Autism Society, 2016a).

HISTORY OF AUTISM

The first occurrence of autism can be dated back to 1799, where an individual—identified in the literature as Victor—presented with characteristics that included the inability to speak, a continuous rocking motion, and an obliviousness to people and sensory stimulation (Webber & Scheuermann, 2008). A French physician named Jean Marc Gaspard Itard took it upon himself to take Victor under his care and teach him social, self-help, cognitive, and communication skills (Webber & Scheuermann, 2008).

In 1943, American–Austrian psychiatrist Leo Kanner explained, through case studies, a condition different than anything reported thus far (Webber & Scheuermann, 2008; Zager, Wehmeyer, & Simpson, 2012). Later identified as infantile autism, the case studies highlighted 11 individuals with cognitive, communication, and affective deficits (Webber & Scheuermann, 2008). It was not until 1980, in the *Diagnostic and Statistical Manual of Mental Disorders* (DSM–III) that infantile autism was acknowledged and identified under pervasive developmental disorder (PDD) (Luiselli et al., 2008; Webber & Scheuermann, 2008).

CHARACTERISTICS OF AUTISM

Autism is a developmental disorder that appears in early childhood and affects communication and social interaction; it occurs across all races, ethnicities, and socioeconomic groups (Centers for Disease Control and Prevention, 2018a). Autism is a spectrum disorder, which means that it varies in severity along a continuum. More specifically, behaviors associated with autism include difficulty with language development, making little or no eye contact, failure to engage in appropriate two-way communication, having intense interests or fixations, poor motor skills, sensory issues, and difficulty with executive functioning (Autism Society, 2016b; Luiselli et al., 2008; U.S. Department of Health and Human Services, 2018; Zager, Wehmeyer, & Simpson, 2012).

According to the fifth edition of the *Diagnostic and Statistical Manual of Mental Disorders* (DSM–5) (American Psychiatric Association, 2017, p. 66), the clinical diagnosis for autism spectrum disorders include

> Persistent deficits in social communication and social interaction across multiple contexts as manifested by the following, currently or by history (examples are illustrative, not exhaustive; see text):
>
> 1. Deficits in social-emotional reciprocity, ranging, for example, from abnormal social approach and failure of normal back-and-forth conversation; to reduced sharing of interests, emotions, or affect; to failure to initiate or respond to social interactions.
> 2. Deficits in nonverbal communicative behaviors used for social interaction, ranging, for example, from poorly integrated verbal and nonverbal communication; to abnormalities in eye contact and body language or deficits

in understanding and use of gestures; to a total lack of facial expressions and nonverbal communication.
3. Deficits in developing, maintaining, and understanding relationships, ranging, for example, from difficulties adjusting behavior to suit various social contexts; to difficulties in sharing imaginative play or in making friends; to absence of interest in peers.

Specify current severity:

Severity is based on social communication impairments and restricted, repetitive patterns of behavior.

Restricted, repetitive patterns of behavior, interests, or activities, as manifested by at least two of the following, currently or by history (examples are illustrative, not exhaustive; see text):

1. Stereotyped or repetitive motor movements, use of objects, or speech (e.g., simple motor stereotypes, lining up toys or flipping objects, echolalia, idiosyncratic phrases).
2. Insistence on sameness, inflexible adherence to routines, or ritualized patterns of verbal or nonverbal behavior (e.g., extreme distress at small changes, difficulties with transitions, rigid thinking patterns, greeting rituals, need to take same route or eat same food every day).
3. Highly restricted, fixated interests that are abnormal in intensity or focus (e.g., strong attachment to or preoccupation with unusual objects, excessively circumscribed or perseverative interests).
4. Hyper- or hypo-reactivity to sensory input or unusual interest in sensory aspects of the environment (e.g., apparent indifference to pain/temperature, adverse response to specific sounds or textures, excessive smelling or touching of objects, visual fascination with lights or movement).

Specify current severity:

Severity is based on social communication impairments and restricted, repetitive patterns of behavior.

Symptoms must be present in the early developmental period (but may not become fully manifested until social demands exceed limited capacities, or may be masked by learned strategies in later life).

Symptoms cause clinically significant impairment in social, occupational, or other important areas of current functioning.

These disturbances are not better explained by intellectual disability (intellectual developmental disorder) or global developmental delay. Intellectual disability and autism spectrum disorder frequently co-occur; to make comorbid diagnoses of autism spectrum disorder and intellectual disability, social communication should be below that expected for general developmental level.

Autism spectrum disorder is the term used to encompass all subtypes of autism. Prior to the DSM–5, autism was divided into separate categories including autistic disorder, Asperger syndrome, childhood disintegrative disorder, and pervasive developmental disorder-not otherwise specified (PDD-NOS) (Special Learning, 2018; Zager, Wehmeyer, & Simpson, 2012). Each subtype, however, has its own unique characteristics.

Autistic disorder is defined as a type of pervasive developmental disorder of abnormal or impaired development prior to age three. The abnormal functioning is present in the areas of psychopathology, reciprocal social interaction, communication, and restrictive and/or repetitive behaviors. This subtype also presents with phobias, disturbances with sleep and eating, and self-directed aggression (Special Learning, 2018; Zager, Wehmeyer, & Simpson, 2012).

Asperger syndrome is a subtype of autism and shares some characteristics such as abnormal social interaction and repetitive interests and behaviors; yet it is vastly different in that it includes normal or above average intelligence without delays in language or cognition (Special Learning 2018; Zager, Wehmeyer, & Simpson, 2012).

PDD-NOS is another subtype of autism that differs as individuals with this diagnosis do not typically fit into any of the other subcategories of autism. Individuals do experience delays, but not in all areas, including communication, social interaction, and restrictive and/or repetitive behaviors (Special Learning, 2018; Zager, Wehmeyer, & Simpson, 2012).

Communication and Language Deficits

Deficits in communication and language development are the most common characteristics of autism. It is estimated that approximately 25%—originally thought to be 50%—of individuals diagnosed with autism never develop speech (Webber & Scheuermann, 2008). Autistic individuals who do develop speech range from nonfunctional communication skills to those similar to typical individuals. It is important to understand that language development and the ability to effectively communicate directly affects cognitive and social development (Webber & Scheuermann, 2008; Zager, Wehmeyer, & Simpson, 2012).

When it comes to communication and language development for individuals with autism, specific terminology applies. *Perseveration*, for example, refers to when an individual repeats words or phrases over and over. *Echolalia* on the other hand, refers to the individual repeating words or phrases said by others without regard to meaning or appropriateness. Further, individuals with autism tend to display very rigid or robotic-like communication. Most communication is extremely literal and consists of short sentences and the overuse of questions (Autism Speaks, 2018a.; Webber & Scheuermann, 2008; Zager, Wehmeyer, & Simpson, 2012).

Social Deficits

Another highly prevalent characteristic of autism includes deficits in social skills, including social interaction, initiating contact, making eye contact, two-way communication, asking for help, and social appropriateness (Zager, Wehmeyer, & Simpson, 2012). In the early years, children with autism prefer to interact with objects rather than other individuals, including caregivers and peers. Autistic children may demonstrate a lack of smiling or making eye contact when engaged in social interactions (Autism Society, 2016c; Webber & Scheuermann, 2008; Zager, Wehmeyer, & Simpson, 2012).

Webber and Scheuermann (2008) discuss the term *joint attention*, which refers to shared social experiences. It is these shared experiences that support language acquisition and social development; however, autistic children do not possess the social cues, such as understanding and responding to facial expressions, to get the benefits of joint attention (Zager, Wehmeyer, & Simpson, 2012). As a result, children with autism are often oblivious to what is going on around them.

Sensory Deficits

Autistic individuals perceive sensory stimuli, including auditory, visual, and tactile, differently than typical individuals; for example, not responding to their name being called or demonstrating extreme reactions to sudden noises are common (Zager, Wehmeyer, & Simpson, 2012). These same individuals tend to have very distinct preferences for certain types of textures, including food and clothing (Webber & Scheuermann, 2008). Other types of stimuli may include lighting, temperature, and room size and layouts (Webber & Scheuermann, 2008; Zager, Wehmeyer, & Simpson, 2012).

Cognitive Deficits

Webber and Scheuermann (2008) highlight the codependence of language in developing cognitive abilities. On the one hand, if cognitive delays are present, it will adversely affect the development of language. On the other hand, if language is impaired then cognitive development will be hindered as language is a critical component for acquiring knowledge (Zager, Wehmeyer, & Simpson, 2012).

There are several cognitive characteristics common in autistic individuals discussed within the literature. The first is referred to as "here-and-now thinking," which supports the understanding that autistic individuals are extremely literal and primarily see the world through their own experiences (Zager, Wehmeyer, & Simpson, 2012). Further, individuals with autism tend to hyperfocus on irrelevant stimuli, often times excluding other important information, which can directly interfere with learning (Webber & Scheuermann, 2008).

Another impeding cognitive characteristic of many autistic individuals is engagement in learning information through rote memorization, which aligns with the knowledge that autistic individuals have very rigid thinking patterns. The problem with rote memorization, according to Webber and Scheuermann (2008), is that it suppresses the ability to open up to new or different ideas or concepts, which hinders the ability to generalize.

Stereotyped Behaviors

Individuals with autism frequently engage in stereotyped behaviors, which may include repetitive movements, such as rocking or spinning, extreme interests and/or preoccupations with very few objects, self-injury or aggressiveness, and tantrums (Zager, Wehmeyer, & Simpson, 2012). Webber and Scheuermann (2008) suggest that these stereotyped behaviors result from a lack of sensory stimulation, which may improve with the appropriate interventions.

DIAGNOSIS OF AUTISM

Although there are no specific medical tests for autism, diagnosis relies heavily on observations relative to communication, social interaction, activities, and interests (Autism Speaks, 2018b). Screenings for autism should occur at regular intervals, suggesting 9 months, 18 months, and 24 months. Early warning signs include not babbling by 12 months; not gesturing, pointing, waving, or grasping by 12 months; not having any singular words by 16 months; not having two-word phrases by 24 months; or having any loss of language or social skills at any age (Autism Speaks, 2018b).

The Centers for Disease Control and Prevention (2018a) acknowledges that children can be diagnosed with autism as early as age two; but most children are diagnosed after age two. Further exploration reveals that the median age for an autism diagnosis is different depending on the subtype to include autistic disorder (3 years and 10 months), PDD-NOS (4 years and 1 month), and Asperger syndrome (6 years and 2 months) (Bleicher, 2013). It is highly recommended, however, that treatment begin as soon as a diagnosis is suspected (U.S. Department of Health and Human Services, 2018).

CAUSES OF AUTISM

There are no known causes of autism; however, several theories have been brought forth, such as genetics, medical problems, heredity, and even vaccinations (Centers for Disease Control and Prevention 2018e). Currently, science has indicated—through imaging—that there are different or abnormal shapes, structures, and functions of the autistic brain (American Speech–Language–Hearing Association 2018). Further, additional research has explored problems during pregnancy or delivery, environmental factors, infections, metabolic imbalances, and exposure to chemicals as possible causes of autism (U.S. Department of Health and Human Services 2018e). Research has confirmed an increase in the occurrence of autism in individuals with certain medical diagnoses, including Fragile X syndrome, tuberous sclerosis complex, congenital rubella syndrome, and untreated phenylketonuria, or PKU (Autism Society, 2015).

CURRENT STATISTICS

Statistics indicate that autism spectrum disorder is the fastest growing developmental disability, with a 119% increase between 2000 and 2010; approximately 35% of young adults age 19 to 23 diagnosed with autism do not have a job or a postsecondary education (Shattuck et al., 2012). Further statistics reveal that autism occurs more frequently in boys than girls, specifically 4.5 times or 1 in 42 boys compared to 1 in 189 girls (Centers for Disease Control and Prevention, 2018c).

FINAL THOUGHTS

Autism is a spectrum disorder that affects communication, social interaction, and behavior. It is considered a spectrum disorder; therefore, the degrees of intensity vary within the characteristics and symptoms (Autism Speaks, 2018b; Autism Society, 2016c; Zager, Wehmeyer, & Simpson, 2012). Research has been extensive in the field trying to uncover a cause for autism; however, these attempts have come up short. Although no direct cause for autism has been identified, researchers have identified atypical brain functioning and comorbid medical diagnoses within autistic individuals (U.S. Department of Health and Human Services, 2018).

Autism is the fourth largest disability category for students receiving special education services within public schools, at 9% (National Center for Educational Statistics, 2016). It is estimated that 1 in 59 individuals are diagnosed with autism within the United States and it occurs at a higher rate in boys as compared to girls (Centers for Disease Control and Prevention,

2018a). Research has highlighted the many benefits of early diagnosis and the immediate start of treatment to improve outcomes for this population of students (Luiselli et al., 2008; Zager, Wehmeyer, & Simpson, 2012).

POINTS TO REMEMBER

- *Autism is a spectrum disorder affecting communication and language development, social interactions, behavior, and sensory stimuli.*
- *Autism occurs at a rate of 1 in 59 individuals within the United States and is the fourth largest category of disabilities served by special education.*
- *Although no direct cause of autism has been identified, research has determined atypical brain development and functioning in those diagnosed with autism, as well as a high rate of comorbid medical conditions.*
- *Prior to the release of the DSM–5, autism was broken down into subcategories. With its release, a diagnosis of autism is now under one broad category encompassing a spectrum of characteristics and symptoms.*

Chapter Two

Protecting and Serving Autistic Individuals

Understanding State and Federal Policies

Autism research has been a fast-growing area in the scientific and educational communities. In 2014, approximately $1.7 billion in federal funding was dedicated to autism research and the development of programs to help provide resources for families of individuals with ASD (Autism Speaks, 2018h). In 2018, an additional bump in funding to the National Institutes of Health guaranteed a greater ability for researchers to continue studying the field of autism and other developmental disabilities.

With the most recent statistics suggesting that 1 in 59 children will receive an autism diagnosis, federal policies and committees have been created to make autism research and funding a priority (Centers for Disease Control and Prevention, 2018a). The Centers for Disease Control and Prevention (CDC) has called autism a national public health crisis that has taken a toll on millions of families (Autism Speaks, 2010). There is no indication of a direct cause and no cure for the disorder at this time, although scientists have suggested that both genetics and environmental factors play a role in its origins (Centers for Disease Control and Prevention, 2018a).

For families, the seeming lack of progress in understanding more about the disability is a major cause of frustration and anger. While families continue to bear the burden of increased financial responsibilities that often result in hardship, the demand for answers, assistance, and a cure remains high (Autism Speaks, 2010). Federal and state governments share these concerns with families and are working diligently to find the answers that families deserve.

Several committees—federal, state, and nonprofit—are currently working on research and services to help families and individuals with ASD to lead more fruitful lives (Centers for Disease Control and Prevention, 2018a; Luterman, 2017). Federal and state governments are also instituting policies that reduce the financial burden on families by covering service costs as well as providing cost-free services and increased access to housing to families who qualify (Autism Speaks, 2018h).

FEDERAL GOVERNMENT RESPONSIBILITIES

The federal government has increased its focus on autism spectrum disorder in many ways. The most obvious is through an increase in the amount of funding provided for researchers who are seeking more information about the disorder; however, the federal government is also working on other initiatives to ensure that individuals with ASD and their families have equal access to programs and services in a similar manner to those with other disabilities (Luterman, 2017; Vohra et al., 2014).

One priority is to improve the outcomes for transition age individuals with ASD on all levels of the spectrum through such initiatives as increasing access to housing and community-based services, making career and technical education more accessible, making sure that educational programs are serving students in the most effective way, increasing the availability of additional postsecondary opportunities for students with ASD, and creating safety resources for independent individuals with ASD (Associated Press, 2017).

Another focus of federal policy is to ensure that all individuals with ASD have access to health care, including related services (Nicolaidis, Kripki, & Raymaker, 2014). Currently, families face many financial roadblocks when it comes to paying for services that are often not covered under insurance plans. Furthermore, gaining access to cost-free, community-based intervention services is difficult at best, and families often experience long wait times which further delays treatment for their child (Nicolaidis, Kripki, & Raymaker, 2014).

At this time, the federal government provides assistance with social security and Medicaid programs that provide waivers for home and community-based services (Nicolaidis, Kripki, & Raymaker, 2014). The hope, however, is that the increased funding in autism research and services will create a wider variety of programs from which individuals with ASD and their families can choose for additional support.

Federal Committees and Policies

Interagency Autism Coordinating Committee (IACC)

The IACC is a federal advisory council designed to coordinate federal efforts on autism research and services (U.S. Department of Health and Human Services, 2018). The committee was originally established in 2000 under the Children's Health Act and has seen many reauthorizations since its inception, the most current under the Autism Collaboration, Accountability, Research, Education, and Support Act of 2014 (U.S. Department of Health and Human Services, 2018). The current committee will remain in effect until 2019 or until reauthorization occurs again (U.S. Department of Health and Human Services, 2018).

The committee is under the supervision of the Office of Autism Research Coordination, a subsidiary of the U.S. Department of Health and Human Services (HHS) (National Institute of Mental Health, 2018). The purpose of the committee is to advise the secretary of HHS on issues regarding the most recent trends in ASD. The committee consists of both federal and public members, ensuring that a wide range of perspectives are heard and understood (U.S. Department of Health and Human Services, 2018).

The mission statement of the IACC, as stated by the U.S. Department of Health and Human Services (2018), purports to provide for the exchange and dissemination of information on ASD as well as the coordination of the various agencies and organizations that provide services for individuals with ASD. The committee also aims to increase the public's understanding of services, research, and public policies on ASD. In 2014, the IACC released its most recent strategic plan, outlining the most relevant concerns of the autism community along with updates addressing them. According to the plan's updated version, a focus on accountability and objectives is key in charting progress on autism interventions and services (Interagency Autism Coordinating Committee, 2014).

The strategic plan outlines seven topics that are of major concern for the public and health care professionals. Topics range from answering parents' questions regarding when they should worry about potential autism symptomatology, to the ways in which the service and research landscape can be broadened to enhance the lives of individuals with ASD (Interagency Autism Coordinating Committee, 2014).

Autism and Developmental Disabilities Monitoring Network (ADDM)

The ADDM is a group of programs funded by the CDC whose aim is to provide an estimate of the number of children living in the United States with ASD and other developmental disabilities (Centers for Disease Control and Prevention, 2018d). The goals of the ADDM include providing a description of the population living with ASD, analysis of the commonalities in diagnoses from the various parts of the country, identification of the changes in the disorder over time, and providing a description of the impact ASD and other developmental disabilities have on various communities nationwide (Centers for Disease Control and Prevention, 2018d).

In 2018, the ADDM published a community report summarizing the findings from the committee's most recent research involving eight-year-old children with ASD (Centers for Disease Control and Prevention, 2018d, f). This report provides schools, parents, and community officials with the most up-to-date findings in autism research. In summary, the ADDM report outlined several key findings based on recent research to include

- One in 59 children are now being identified as having an ASD.
- ASD diagnoses were lowest in Arkansas (1 in 77) and highest in New Jersey (1 in 34).
- Boys were four times more likely to be identified as being on the spectrum than girls. Additionally, white children are more likely to be identified as having ASD than either black or Hispanic children.
- Approximately 42% of children diagnosed with autism were evaluated by the age of three.
- Nearly 1/3 of the students studied who had IQ scores available for analysis also qualified as a student with an intellectual disability (Centers for Disease Control and Prevention, 2018d).

These findings are based on populations in 11 states and, as such, may not be indicative of experiences in other states. They will, however, likely have a tremendous impact on the way in which schools and service providers work with autistic individuals; for example, knowing that less than half of all students studied were evaluated by the age of three will hopefully influence both state and federal programs to create initiatives that develop more comprehensive and timely processes for early screening and detection of ASD (Centers for Disease Control and Prevention, 2018d).

Centers for Autism and Developmental Disabilities Research and Epidemiology (CADDRE)

Like the ADDM, the CADDRE's goals are to monitor the number of children with ASD and other developmental disabilities; however, the CADDRE also aims to conduct epidemiological research on developmental disorders in order to further the knowledge about potential factors influencing a positive diagnosis (Centers for Disease Control and Prevention, 2018e). The California Center for Autism and Developmental Disabilities Research, one of the largest branches of CADDRE, has been analyzing medical records of autistic children in order to examine potential risk factors during pregnancy and early childhood (Autism Speaks, 2018d).

One particularly important study funded by the CDC is the Study to Explore Early Development (SEED). SEED is currently the largest study in the United States whose aim is to identify factors that may put children at risk for developing autism (Centers for Disease Control and Prevention, 2018g). The study currently includes children from ages two to five years who participate in one of three study groups: children with ASD, children with other developmental disabilities, and children without developmental disabilities.

SEED research sites are currently in six states (Colorado, Georgia, Maryland, Missouri, North Carolina, and Wisconsin), with the data processing center in Michigan. According to CADDRE's description of the scientific goals of SEED, the study aims to characterize the behavioral phenotype of ASD as well as investigate the genetic and environmental risk factors associated with ASD and other developmental disabilities, with a focus on immunological, hormonal, gastrointestinal, and socioeconomic characteristics (Centers for Disease Control and Prevention, 2018g; Schendel et al., 2012).

The outcomes of this study will be helpful in interpreting previously gathered data as well as targeting areas that can be examined in the next generation of studies. The existence of a lab that houses biological specimens of individuals with ASD may be useful in testing new treatments in the future (Schendel et al., 2012).

STATE PRIORITIES

State governments are following federal mandates by increasing attention to ASD and related disabilities. For individuals who are insured through state-level health care coverage, state governments are working to ensure that autism treatment is covered under these insurance plans as well as addressing any gaps in services that may not be covered by existing insurance plans (Nicolaidis, Kripki, & Raymaker, 2014).

States are following the example set by federal policies to ensure that transition-age individuals with ASD have access to housing, employment, and training by carefully examining and eliminating wait lists for home- and community-based services to ensure that all individuals with ASD have timely access to the services they need (Associated Press, 2017).

States are reexamining the current resources for students with ASD in schools. In order to ensure that school-based services are being delivered with fidelity and in the most effective manner, states are looking at the training needs of staff, especially those who work with students who have enhanced needs such as augmentative and alternative communication (AAC), and behavioral and sensory needs (The Conversation, 2018).

Many educators lack the proper training to work with autistic students; thus, it is essential that more resources are devoted to providing professional development opportunities within schools (Higginson & Chatfield, 2012). States have realized that educators are a major piece of the support system for students with ASD and their families. Without state- and federal-level support it is unlikely that schools will be able to provide quality services for students that need it the most (Higginson & Chatfield, 2012).

Federal and state governments share responsibility in many of the programs and acts created to better the lives of autistic individuals. One such act, the Achieving a Better Life Experience Act (ABLE), was signed into law in 2014 (Autism Speaks, 2018f). This act creates federal tax law provisions that enable families to set up tax-exempt savings accounts that will help with the postsecondary costs for individuals with ASD and other disabilities (Autism Speaks, 2018f; National Disability Institute, 2018).

The bill supplements existing programs and services without interfering in current service delivery. States are mandated to incorporate ABLE into all of their programs (Autism Speaks, 2018f). This allows for broader access to services such as housing, education, and transportation, without the worry that the savings accounts will be viewed as extra income and, thus, impact income qualifications for many of the services that individuals with ASD may already have in place (Autism Speaks, 2018f; National Disability Institute, 2018).

State Committees and Policies

Individual states have created their own committees, as well as enacted their own policies in order to bring autism awareness to the forefront. A brief sampling of state programs available to help with diagnosing and servicing autistic individuals shows the breadth of available services. Many state-level programs are involved in federal studies, providing data for broader autism outreach.

Massachusetts Autism Commission

In 2014, Massachusetts enacted the Autism Omnibus Law, which established the Autism Commission. This body of 35 members has the task of making recommendations on policies that impact individuals with ASD (Commonwealth of Massachusetts, 2018). The committee also serves to investigate the range of services needed by individuals with ASD that will help them to experience success throughout their lives. Some of the areas in which the commission works include public education, higher education, employment, independent living, social opportunities, and housing (Commonwealth of

Massachusetts, 2018). Additionally, the Autism Commission develops plans of action based on the needs of individuals on the autism spectrum that are founded on data and research.

Michigan Autism Council

Created in 2012, the Michigan Autism Council works under the umbrella of the Michigan Department of Health and Human Services in order to advise other entities on the needs of individuals with ASD. The council works to support the development of autism-specific legislation (Michigan Autism Program, 2018). Members of the council regularly review trends in autism, progress on research, and heavy needs areas for individuals with ASD. The goal of the council is to keep up with the latest research in autism so that improved recommendations can be made for state and local services.

Autism Society of North Carolina (ASNC)

The ASNC aims to provide support for individuals and families affected by ASD. They focus on a community-based service model, putting parents in touch with various services to help support them on their journey. The society purports to have helped lower the average age of diagnosis below the national average (Autism Society of North Carolina, 2018). The ASNC's goal is to provide direct service to families and individuals with ASD through increased advocacy, development of programs for underserved regions, and ensuring that wraparound services are provided for individuals who have intense needs (Autism Society of North Carolina, 2018).

Other Organizations Working with State and Federal Programs

In addition to the many state and federal programs and committees working on improvements for autism awareness, there are several privately funded or donor-funded organizations that support both state and federal policies as well as help spread awareness and knowledge to the public.

Autism Speaks

Autism Speaks is perhaps one of the most widely recognized organizations providing autism awareness and support resources. It operates worldwide and was founded on the premise that a better understanding of autism can lead to improved outcomes for individuals and families struggling with the disorder (Autism Speaks, 2018e). Autism Speaks was founded in 2005 by Bob and Suzanne Wright, grandparents of an autistic child; it was backed financially by a $25 million donation from Bernard "Bernie" Marcus, an American businessman who recognized the need for more research and support for such a prevalent disorder (Autism Speaks, 2018e).

The vision of the organization is to advance research into the causes of autism, as well as better treatment options for individuals who have been diagnosed with ASD (Autism Speaks, 2018e). Autism Speaks has worked, and continues to work, with federal and state agencies to better understand the causes of autism, provide increased access to appropriate intervention, assist families with banks of information about the disorder, and provide updated lists of resources for families and individuals (Autism Speaks, 2018e). The organization exists on donations gained from fundraisers, such as the Autism Speaks Walk, which occurs in various locations throughout the United States.

National Autism Association (NAA)

Similar to Autism Speaks, the NAA aims to provide education and resources for families with autistic members. The NAA promotes advocacy for individuals on the spectrum as well as provides empowerment for families through shared stories and support from others with similar experiences (National Autism Association, 2018). The NAA also provide training opportunities to first responders and service professionals, which is especially important for understanding how to handle the needs of an autistic individual during a crisis. For schools, the NAA has a host of tools that it can provide, ranging from sensory needs to teaching students with ASD about safety and well-being (National Autism Association, 2018).

Autism Science Foundation

Founded in 2009, the Autism Science Foundation's focus is on the science behind autism. The nonprofit organization supports autism research at all levels by providing scientists with assistance in conducting autism research. This includes all phases of research from experimental design through publication and dissemination of information (Autism Science Foundation, 2018). The foundation is a supporter of scientific research and has been outspoken about the failed vaccine causation theory. Although still controversial, it is the hope that increased research will uncover clear indicators of ASD likelihood.

FINAL THOUGHTS

While autism research will likely continue for many years before a cause and cure are discovered, there are several programs and organizations that support the journey. Federal and state programs and policies enacted to increase awareness of ASD have seen an explosion of success in their missions and continue to work diligently to increase access to services for families with autistic children. Federal and state priorities have aligned as the end goal for everyone involved in autism activism, to gain better knowledge so more effective treatment options and resources can be created and made available to families.

In addition to federal and state programs, nonprofit organizations are also leading the way in the fight against autism. These agencies work collaboratively with governmental committees to connect families with the latest trends in research. As nonprofit organizations, they are in a unique position to direct their research toward the needs of their supporters. However, many of the nonprofit organizations currently studying autism have aligned forces with federally funded research in order to provide the best chance at combating the disorder.

Although the world may not see results of this research for decades to come, the work and dedication of federal, state, and nonprofit organizations will continue to increase the quality of life for families and individuals with autism by turning it from a stigma into an exceptionality.

POINTS TO REMEMBER

- *In 2014, approximately $1.7 billion in federal funding was dedicated to autism research and the development of programs to help provide resources for families of individuals with ASD (Autism Speaks, 2018e).*
- *Both federal and state governments have prioritized autism research in order to improve the lives of families and individuals with ASD.*
- *Federal committees such as the IAAC, ADDM, and CADDRE are working tirelessly to make gains in autism research and the provision of resources.*
- *States often have their own individual autism councils that work with federal committees to disseminate information to communities as well as to provide data to federal research organizations to help in the fight against autism.*
- *Nonprofit organizations such as Autism Speaks have increased autism awareness around the world.*

Chapter Three

Creating the Foundation for Success in Students with Autism

From Assessment to Educational Goals

Autism spectrum disorder (ASD) has garnered much attention in recent years as an increased number of individuals have been diagnosed with the disability. Children and adults who are diagnosed with ASD commonly have deficits in socialization, in addition to demonstrating restricted, repetitive behaviors or activities; however, not all individuals on the autism spectrum show the same disability characteristics (Asaro-Saddler et al., 2015). There is also a vast variability in terms of language development, intellectual ability, and adaptive functioning (Asaro-Saddler et al., 2015). Students with ASD may need minimal support, or they may require substantial assistance in order to experience success within the classroom. Depending upon the student's level of need, there is a push for students with ASD to be educated in general education classrooms to the greatest extent possible as defined in the Individuals with Disabilities Education Act (IDEA) (Lee, 2018; U.S. Department of Education, 2010). Yet not all teachers understand the implications of teaching a student with ASD, and many educators are not specifically trained in working with students on the spectrum. It is important for educators to develop a solid awareness of the process of identifying the probability of ASD as well as the ways in which an autism diagnosis can impact instructional practices.

Chapter 3
DIAGNOSING AUTISM

In order to determine the best supports and interventions, it is necessary to first understand the ways in which autism diagnoses have changed over recent years. The DSM–5 has made significant changes to the diagnostic criteria for ASD (Wong & Koh, 2016). Looking at the *Diagnostic and Statistical Manual for Mental Disorders, Fourth Edition* (DSM–IV), the categories of Asperger's syndrome, CDD, and PDD-NOS have all been collected and placed under the broader heading of ASD in the new version of the manual (Wong & Koh, 2016).

The newer DSM–5 has only two categories of impairment that must be present in ASD—as opposed to the three categories previously stated in the DSM–IV—social communication deficits and restricted and repetitive behaviors. Along with the changes to the diagnostic criteria, the DSM–5 provides severity levels in order to more accurately interpret the individual's symptoms (Wong & Koh, 2016). Researchers have suggested that early diagnosis with valid diagnostic processes is key in providing children with early interventions that are both needed and appropriate (Vllasaliu et al., 2016).

Diagnostic Instruments

There are several common diagnostic assessments when questioning an ASD diagnosis. These assessments are a mix of interviews, observations, and rating scales that can be filled out by individuals who have intimate knowledge of the student in question. The success of many of these commonly used instruments is based on the level of experience the clinician or parent has with symptoms of ASD (Vllasaliu et al., 2016). It is important to note that none of the instruments presented here are representative of objectively obtained data and so the scientific validity of the results cannot be guaranteed in all cases. Presented as follows are the five most commonly utilized assessments in diagnosing ASD.

The Autism Diagnostic Interview–Revised (ADI–R)

The ADI–R consists of a semistructured interview process that contains 93 items related to behavior corresponding to different ages (Vllasaliu et al., 2016). These items are rated on a scale of zero to three; however, additional scoring options are available for answers such as "not applicable" or "not known or not asked." For example, zero would equal behavior not present, while three would equal extreme severity of the behavior (Vllasaliu et al., 2016).

This assessment is administered by a clinician who interviews parents and/or caretakers who have intimate knowledge of a child's developmental history and current behavior patterns (Pearson Clinical, 2017). The probability of autism is determined through ratings on interview questions rather than on nationally normed scales (Pearson Clinical, 2017). The ADI–R was developed to be used in conjunction with the Autism Diagnostic Observation Schedule (ADOS) to create a valid diagnosis for the probability of ASD (Le Couteur et al., 2008).

The Autism Diagnostic Observation Schedule (ADOS)

The ADOS is an assessment that uses direct observation to assess the presence of ASD in children and adolescents (Le Couteur et al., 2008). A trained clinician is the only individual who can complete the ADOS, and here the clinician uses a semistructured observation and interview protocol that assesses the likelihood that the behavior displayed by the subject fits the ASD cutoff criteria (Vllasaliu et al., 2016). During the ADOS, the clinician engages the subject in standardized play scenarios that assess the individual's levels of communication and social reciprocity.

There are four different modules of the ADOS available depending upon the subject's level of communication proficiency (Vllasaliu et al., 2016). In order to diagnose the probability of ASD, the clinician scores the assessment according to a set of module-specific algorithms (Luyster et al., 2009). This particular assessment is viewed as the "gold standard" among education professionals, although its effectiveness with very young children is uncertain (Luyster et al., 2009).

The Diagnostic Interview for Social and Communication Disorders (DISCO)

Another of the interview-type instruments used to diagnose the presence of an autism spectrum disorder is the DISCO. This assessment consists of over 300 questions that are asked of a parent and/or caretaker; 93 are diagnostic questions and of those 38 items assess the presence of impairments in social interaction, 15 items assess the presence of impairments in communications, and 29 items assess the presence of stereotyped behaviors (Vllasaliu et al., 2016). While this assessment does not have age restrictions like many other assessments, it can be used to diagnose a wide variety of disabilities such as psychiatric disorders and other developmental disabilities (Vllasaliu et al., 2016).

The Asperger Syndrome Diagnostic Interview (ASDI)

The ASDI consists of a short, standardized set of interview questions that are presented to a parent and/or caretaker. Ideally, the interviewee would have known the child in question during infancy in order to best answer the questions asked in the assessment (Vllasaliu et al., 2016). The ASDI is divided into six categories of items: impairment in social interaction, restricted interests, routines, verbal and speech problems, nonverbal communication problems, and motor clumsiness (Vllasaliu et al., 2016). The items are then rated on a scale of one (does not apply) to three (definitely applies). If one item in each category is rated positively, then it is determined that a diagnosis of Asperger's syndrome is present (Vllasaliu et al., 2016).

Gilliam Autism Rating Scale–Third Edition (GARS–3)

The GARS–3 is a norm-referenced assessment used to screen for the probability of ASD (Karren, 2016). This assessment can be used with individuals between the ages of three and twenty-two years (Pearson Clinical, 2017). The instrument is composed of six subcategories that were created in accordance with the new diagnostic criteria from the DSM–5 (Karren, 2016). The subcategories include restricted and repetitive behaviors, social interaction, social communication, emotional responses, cognitive style, and maladaptive speech.

A trained individual must score the assessment, although the rating scales are given to teachers, parents, and other caregivers who have intimate knowledge and sustained interaction with the child who is being assessed (Karren 2016). This assessment only provides the clinician with subjective information that proposes the likelihood or probability that a student may have ASD. Caution must be taken to ensure that the individuals who fill out the rating scales are chosen based on their knowledge of the child and not based solely on their availability to answer the questions.

THE IMPACT OF ASD ON INSTRUCTION

Individuals with ASD can experience struggles with focus and sustaining attention on tasks (Finn et al., 2015). Additionally, those with ASD can have difficulty with executive functioning skills, such as time management, self-monitoring, creating a plan of action for a task, and even rapid memory retrieval (Finn et al., 2015). In most individuals without disabilities, executive functioning skills develop naturally; however, for individuals with ASD the level of support and intervention needed can be overwhelming for educators who have little training in meeting the needs of students on the autism spectrum.

Children with ASD can also experience difficulty with fine motor skills and visual-motor speed, which can greatly impact skills such as handwriting or typing (Asaro-Saddler et al., 2015). This can negatively impact the student's progress in the classroom since generally the student's writing will be briefer and more difficult to read. When writing is illegible, it can lead to lower scores on written assignments, causing a lower grade for the student than may be warranted (Asaro-Saddler et al., 2015).

Another area that can be a profound struggle for students on the autism spectrum is functional speech. While many educators think of ASD as a disability affecting social skills, it is critical to become cognizant of students who are nonverbal. Students who lack functional speech rely on physical behaviors, such as pointing and facial expressions, and often more aggressive behaviors such as hitting and throwing objects, in order to get their needs met (Xin & Leonard, 2014).

For this subset of student, behaviors can become difficult to manage and frustrations continue to grow as it becomes more challenging for educators to understand student requests. While there are many teachers and other professionals who are adept at understanding the function of behavior, the goal of educating these individuals is to provide them with the skills to become independently able to communicate at a functional level.

Increasing Executive Functioning Skills

As previously mentioned, individuals with ASD can experience difficulties with attention and executive functioning skills. Promoting self-monitoring as a means of helping the student become aware of the necessity to perform a specific task can be helpful in developing independence in students with ASD. Self-monitoring is a skill that students can utilize to ensure that they are performing daily living tasks, managing their time effectively, and meeting deadlines (Finn et al., 2015). Individuals with a variety of disabilities can benefit from self-monitoring techniques; however, it is important to note that they must be used in conjunction with other methods of increasing executive functioning skills as there is not one standalone practice that has been found to be effective in all instances (Finn et al., 2015).

Not all students with ASD have the same executive functioning deficits; thus, it is necessary to provide students with self-monitoring techniques that can be tailored to their individual needs. Tactile prompting devices are especially helpful in that they can discreetly alert the student to a needed transition (Anson, Todd, & Casseretto, 2008). One such device, called WatchMinder, has had success in several research studies in promoting student independence for following routines and completing tasks (Finn et al., 2015).

WatchMinder is a vibrating, programmable wristwatch-like device that can be customized depending on the student's unique needs (WatchMinder, 2018). Researchers have used this device for a variety of tasks from assisting adults with traumatic brain injuries with taking medication on time, to helping individuals with intellectual disabilities with task management and completion (Finn et al., 2015; Green, Hughes, & Ryan, 2011).

Another tool that can be beneficial in helping students with ASD develop better self-monitoring skills is called MotivAider (Behavioral Dynamics, 2018). The MotivAider is a pager-like device that users can either clip to their pants or wear in their pocket. The device works much like a traditional pager in the sense that it will vibrate when the user's attention is needed (Behavioral Dynamics, 2018; Finn et al., 2015).

Similar to the WatchMinder, the MotivAider allows the user to set customized messages through either text or images that work to remind and motivate the individual to engage in a desired behavior (Behavioral Dynamics, 2018; WatchMinder, 2018). The benefit to students who use either form of self-monitoring tool is that they can become increasingly independent by learning to set up their own devices and follow through on the reminders (Finn et al., 2015).

Increasing Written Expression Skills

Writing is a fundamental skill that is necessary in order to communicate with others in a variety of settings; however, for individuals with ASD, writing can be an extremely challenging task that takes exponential effort to complete (Asaro-Saddler et al., 2015). School-aged children with ASD have even greater challenges since the increased focus on standardized testing requires that students write more than ever before.

It is important, therefore, to recognize that writing may be difficult for individuals on the autism spectrum for reasons that are not solely related to fine motor deficits. Individuals with ASD may also struggle with the ability to maintain the organization necessary to write a coherent piece, or they may have deficits in understanding how to appropriately write for different audiences (Asaro-Saddler et al., 2015).

Students with ASD who demonstrate compromised executive functioning abilities may also experience weaknesses in central coherence. Weak central coherence is thought to contribute to difficulties in writing by way of interfering with the individual's ability to see the broader picture, therefore, creating an inability to plan and execute a coherent written composition (Asaro-Saddler et al., 2015; Carnahan, Williamson, & Christman, 2011). This can impact not only the academic progress of students with ASD, but also their self-esteem, ability to gain employment, and capacity to communicate wants and needs on paper.

Another area in which individuals with ASD struggle is understanding the ways in which to write for different target audiences. Because individuals with ASD often struggle to understand others' feelings and perceptions, writing for an absent audience is extremely difficult. Additionally, attempting to explain the thoughts, motivation, and feelings of characters is also very challenging for individuals with ASD (Asaro-Saddler et al., 2015).

This difficulty is due in part to deficits in theory of mind. Theory of mind is the principle that "refers to our understanding of people as mental beings, each with his or her own mental states—such as thoughts, wants, motives, and feelings" (Astington & Edward, 2010, p. 1). For students with ASD, the inability to understand others' perspectives makes it difficult to write about someone who thinks in a different manner (Asaro-Saddler et al., 2015).

It is not surprising that educators face challenges when providing writing instruction for students on the autism spectrum; however, it is important to keep in mind that students with ASD have many strengths that can help them overcome their writing deficits. Students with ASD, for example, are often fluent in the use of technology (Asaro-Saddler et al., 2015).

Tapping into the student's interest in technology can help improve student outcomes in the writing process. Allowing the use of computers to aid in the writing process can help the student focus on the formulation of ideas instead of on struggling to maintain control over both the cognition of writing and the physical act of forming letters and sentences (Asaro-Saddler et al., 2015; Carnahan, Williamson, & Christman, 2011).

Some students need more assistance to improve their writing skills than simply the provision of technology. Researchers are beginning to explore the efficacy of available software that assists students with ASD to become independent writers (Asaro-Saddler et al., 2015). One such software program, First Author, has shown promise with regard to helping students to plan and develop written pieces on both special interest topics and curriculum-based assignments (Asaro-Saddler et al., 2015).

The program works by prompting students to choose a topic about which to write, along with a picture cue. The program guides students through the writing process by providing accommodations such as word banks, word prediction, and immediate auditory feedback (Asaro-Saddler et al., 2015). Programs like this can be helpful in encouraging students to begin the writing process, while also helping them to become better able to successfully plan a writing piece from start to finish.

Increasing Communication Skills

Many individuals with ASD present with little to no verbal speech ability. In order to communicate, they rely on physical behaviors to convey their needs. Often that behavior can become aggressive and violent. With the aim of assisting individuals with ASD to develop functional communication skills, augmentative and alternative communication (AAC) devices have been shown to increase the individual's ability to convey his or her needs in a way that closely resembles functional speech (Xin & Leonard, 2014).

Many AAC devices use pictures, symbols, and other visual means to communicate the student's thoughts (Xin & Leonard, 2014). In addition to allowing the student to communicate with others, these devices can be helpful in the acquirement of new vocabulary. New concepts and words can be added to the device to help students learn new language using a method that is consistent and familiar (Xin & Leonard, 2014).

There are many types of AAC devices on the market, and it is important to choose a device that is most effective for the student. One AAC option, speech generating devices (SGDs), allow students to press a symbol and have it generated into audible speech (Xin & Leonard, 2014). SGDs are especially effective in helping students to increase their interactions with peers and teachers within the classroom (Boyd, Hart Barnett, & More, 2015; Shane et al., 2012).

Recent development of improved SGDs includes applications for the iPad, which are relatively cost-friendly, small in size, and can be used in virtually every situation. These devices are increasingly being used in general education classrooms to include nonverbal students with ASD with their nondisabled peers (Shane et al., 2012; Xin & Leonard, 2014). The iPad made it easier for teachers to monitor students' progress with language and skill development as well as to keep students engaged in learning (Xin & Leonard, 2014).

In addition to tracking students' learning, AAC devices such as the iPad can increase the student's ability to develop social skills. Social learning is especially crucial for students with ASD. Improving opportunities for students with ASD to communicate with nondisabled peers can increase the potential to become included in the general school community; therefore, opening up more options for inclusion throughout the course of their school years and beyond (Boyd, Hart Barnett, & More, 2015; Xin & Leonard, 2014).

AAC devices may also be helpful in creating a better understanding of the strengths of individuals with ASD. Many people believe that individuals with ASD do not understand speech in the same way as their typically developed peers. In many cases, the student with ASD has strong receptive language skills; however, the student has difficulty with expressive language skills (Xin & Leonard, 2014). AAC devices can act as a bridge, creating opportunities for increased social reciprocity and decreased aggressive behavior (Boyd, Hart Barnett, & More, 2015).

Interventions Involving Game Play

In a society that relies on rapidly changing technology for entertainment purposes, there is an emerging body of research that suggests that this same technology can be used to target specific skill deficits in students with ASD (Whyte, Smyth, & Scherf, 2014). Software developers are moving toward "serious games" as a means of increasing intrinsic motivation and cognitive functioning in individuals with psychosocial and developmental disorders (Whyte, Smyth, & Scherf, 2014). Serious games are defined as games that are "designed to foster learning of targeted skills that are particularly difficult and not rewarding for participants" (Whyte, Smyth, & Scherf, 2014, p. 3821). The goal in these games is to take the learning from the game and generalize it into real life. In order to help facilitate this generalization, serious games utilize the principles of standard video game design to create an enjoyable and entertaining form of game play, while employing theories from field or learning and development (Whyte, Smyth, & Scherf, 2014).

Although these games are not well known to most in the gaming world, serious games are emerging as a way to blend the virtual world with real life. One such serious game, for example, called *Re-Mission*, is a project of Hope-Lab, a nonprofit that harnesses the power and appeal of technology to improve human health and well-being (HopeLab, 2018). The purpose of the game is to help kids and young adults with cancer fight back (HopeLab, 2018).

Based on scientific research, the games provide cancer support by giving players a sense of power and control, while encouraging treatment adherence (Burak & Parker, 2017). A game such as *Re-Mission* gives players some agency over their condition in the virtual world while helping them to manage their symptoms in the real world.

With regard to students on the autism spectrum, one such serious game that has shown promise with increasing social skills is *FaceSay* (Symbionica, n.d.). *FaceSay* is a social skills serious game that is thought to improve social interactions between students with ASD and their nondisabled peers (Symbionica, n.d.). The aim of the game is to increase the student's emotional and facial recognition skills through a series of visuals (Symbionica, n.d.).

Players receive points for correct answers when asked to perform such tasks as determine facial emotions, follow eye gaze, and recognize facial features of different individuals. A study in which children and adolescents with autism ages 6 to 15 completed a six-week trial of *FaceSay* showed that these subjects did indeed improve their facial and emotional recognition skills (Whyte, Smyth, & Scherf, 2014).

Developing skills that can be utilized in situations other than the playground is important for increasing social understanding among autistic individuals. Virtual reality platforms have been developed with the purpose of generalizing skills from the computer-based environment to real-world social interactions (Whyte, Smyth, & Scherf, 2014). These games use social stories and feedback with the aim of training autistic individuals how to deal with increasingly complex social interactions, such as negotiating with a salesperson or interviewing for a job (Whyte, Smyth, & Scherf, 2014). The ultimate goal of serious games is that individuals with autism will be able to transfer these skills into real-life social situations, such as increased conversational skills and the ability to navigate social interactions independently.

FINAL THOUGHTS

As ASD diagnoses have risen over the years, educators have been slow to receive training in this area. In order for educators to create more effective teaching practices designed to address the many areas of need for autistic individuals, they must first understand that all autistic children do not present the same; thus, the needs of each child will be as different as they are. Individuals with ASD have diverse strengths and weaknesses similar to their typically developed counterparts.

Fortunately, in recent years, the goal of helping individuals on the autism spectrum become more included in the general population has been the drive behind some of the new and innovative assistive technology practices targeting autistic individuals. It is crucial for educators to become aware of the existence of these options in order to better plan for working with their autistic students. With the push toward inclusion, more and more students with ASD will receive their education with their typically developed peers; however, one cannot deny that each autistic student will need some varying degree of support.

In order to create the best plan, educators must avail themselves of both the diagnostic measures of determining autism as well as the assistive technology tools that are available to help students with ASD increase their communication and executive functioning skills. While this chapter does not contain an exhaustive list of technology options, it is a starting point for interested educators toward more options for intervention and skill building.

POINTS TO REMEMBER

- *Children and adults who are diagnosed with autism spectrum disorder (ASD) commonly have deficits in socialization, in addition to demonstrating restricted, repetitive behaviors or activities (Asaro-Saddler et al., 2015).*
- *Often there is a vast variability in terms of language development, intellectual ability, and adaptive functioning among individuals with ASD (Asaro-Saddler et al., 2015).*
- *Autism is often diagnosed through a mix of commonly used diagnostic assessments that are completed by the parent and/or patient (if applicable) and scored by a clinician.*

- *Individuals with ASD can have difficulty with executive functioning skills, such as time management, self-monitoring, creating a plan of action for a task, and even rapid memory retrieval (Finn et al., 2015).*
- *The goal of helping individuals on the autism spectrum become more included in the general population has been the drive behind some of the new and innovative assistive technology practices targeting autistic individuals.*
- *In order to create the best educational plan, educators must avail themselves of both the diagnostic measures of determining autism as well as the assistive technology tools that are available to help students with ASD increase their communication and executive functioning skills.*

Chapter Four

Developing Effective Educational Programs for Autistic Students

Challenges and Solutions

Autism spectrum disorder (ASD) has quickly become one of the fastest growing categories of disability in the United States. According to the Centers for Disease Control and Prevention (2018b), the prevalence of an autism diagnosis has increased from 1 in 150 children in 2000, to 1 in 59 children in 2014. ASD has been reported in all racial, ethnic, and socioeconomic groups, and is four times more common among males than among females (Centers for Disease Control and Prevention, 2018c). Of the children diagnosed with a developmental disability, impairments can range from mild concerns requiring little intervention to severe concerns that require intense support services from a multitude of providers (Centers for Disease Control and Prevention, 2018c).

An autism diagnosis cannot be made with a blood test or other medical test, but rather is diagnosed through behavior observations and subjective rating scales that when scored indicate the likelihood of the presence of ASD. Interestingly, public schools have been the primary diagnosticians for the probability of ASD in school-aged children (Ruble & McGrew, 2013).

The number of children with autism serviced in public schools has risen from 94,000 in 2000 to over 400,000 in 2011 (Kuo, 2016). Public schools continue to be the only publicly funded institution to be mandated by federal law to ensure that all students receive a free and appropriate public education (FAPE) regardless of socioeconomic background (Ruble & McGrew, 2013).

One major challenge in providing FAPE to students with ASD is a lack of understanding of the best ways in which to develop meaningful, beneficial educational programming (Anglim, Prendeville, & Kinsella, 2017; Ruble & McGrew, 2013). Morrier, Hess, and Heflin (2011) found that out of 90 teachers trained in instructional practices for autistic students, only 5% reported using these strategies. Additionally, a lack of understanding of effective educational programming and supports for students with ASD can lead to poor-quality individualized education programs (IEPs) (Ruble et al., 2010).

CHALLENGES TO EFFECTIVE IMPLEMENTATION OF EDUCATIONAL PROGRAMMING

Teaching Factors

The Individuals with Disabilities Education Act of 2004 (IDEA) indicates that students with disabilities should be educated to the maximum extent appropriate alongside their nondisabled peers. With the aim of ensuring that students with ASD are receiving effective interventions and supports in the least restrictive environment (LRE), teachers and other educational support staff must be trained in and willing to use research-based strategies (Koegel et al., 2012; Morrier, Hess, & Heflin, 2011).

Teacher training, beyond what is received in college programs, varies between districts (Anglim, Prendeville, & Kinsella, 2017). This can make it difficult to ensure consistency in practices among schools that may be geographically close, but are not under the same superintendence. In order to determine the best interventions for each individual student, teachers and support staff must understand the critical need for accurate data collection (Koegel et al., 2012).

Data collection is key in discovering the most effective interventions for a student with ASD. Because autism is mainly characterized by a lack of communication and social skills, it is important that educators begin with these two domains when determining appropriate programming (Koegel et al., 2012). Students with ASD often display challenging behaviors in place of communication skills, which in turn limits these students' success in developing meaningful social interactions with peers (Koegel et al., 2012). Without appropriate and consistent data collection that can be analyzed over a period of time, educators cannot develop an effective plan of action to help with the development of new skills that can be generalized across environments (Ruble et al., 2010).

Another obstacle related to teachers' understanding of working with students with ASD has to do with their own belief system surrounding the use of appropriate interventions. Koegel et al. (2012) cite a study in which teachers' perceptions surrounding research-based interventions were examined. Results suggest that many teachers did not view an intervention as being research based as important criteria when choosing the most effective intervention for their students (Koegel et al., 2012). Interestingly, many teachers planned which interventions they would use based on personal beliefs (Boardman et al., 2005).

In many instances, teachers choose interventions based on their perception of a student's ability, level of support needed, and availability of resources. If an intervention does not fit into the planned curriculum, it is often not chosen, or it is changed so that its effectiveness is hindered (Koegel et al., 2012). Based on this finding, continued training opportunities surrounding research-based interventions are critical in helping educators to effectively support students with ASD.

Assessment Factors

With educational standards that are more stringent than ever before, standardized testing has become the norm for students in U.S. schools; however, students with disabilities, particularly ASD, often have difficulty meeting proficiency scores on standardized exams (Koegel et al., 2012). As students move from elementary to middle school to high school, the curriculum becomes increasingly more complex, creating a need for more targeted and often intense accommodations and instructional strategies (Test, Smith, & Carter, 2014). Basing levels of mastery on standardized tests alone is extremely problematic for students with ASD because they often have trouble maintaining focus, behaving appropriately, or simply understanding the questions asked on the assessment.

Koegel et al. (2012) suggest that educators employ criterion-based or observation-based assessments in addition to standardized assessments in order to gain useful information about a student's level of progress. In these types of assessments, objective information can be gained and data can be collected in order to measure progress on the student's educational goals as outlined in the student's IEP.

Utilizing multiple types of assessments can provide the educator with a broader picture of the student's abilities, making programmatic planning easier and more effective (Koegel et al., 2012). Research suggests that when a student with ASD is provided with strong instruction, rigorous educational opportunities, differentiated assessments, and personalized supports, the student is more likely to reach his or her potential and, in many cases, go on to postsecondary education and careers (Test, Smith, & Carter, 2014).

IEP Factors

According to the IDEA (2006), "the term individualized education program or IEP means a written statement for each child with a disability that is developed, reviewed, and revised in a meeting in accordance with 34 CFR

300.320 through 300.324" (p. 1). Briefly, the IEP must include (1) the student's present levels of performance, (2) measurable annual goals, (3) a description of alternate assessments, if applicable, (4) a statement of special education, related services, and supplementary aids and services that are being provided to the student, and (5) a statement regarding any individual accommodations that are necessary to measure the student's academic and functional achievement (IDEA, 2006; Ruble et al., 2010).

Due to either a lack of training on how to appropriately construct an IEP, or through a lack of effort to determine the most appropriate plan for the student, IEPs for students with ASD are, in many cases, not meeting the requirements set forth under the IDEA (Ruble et al., 2010). One of the biggest challenges for executing an effective IEP is a lack of understanding on how to write a measurable goal.

For students with ASD, teams often fail to consider the unique concerns associated with autism such as functional communication, social reciprocity, and executive functioning skills (Szidon, Ruppar, & Smith, 2015). This may lead to goals that are written to measure passive participation in the objectives, are specific to a given curriculum and therefore are not generalizable to real life, or only measure episodic events that do not occur with consistency (Szidon et al., 2015).

With regard to academic goals, many IEPs contain objectives that attempt to only measure the student's ability to meet the state curriculum standards. Even though the team may feel that the student has the potential to meet a particular standard without much support, teams must take into consideration the need for academic goals that are individualized specifically to the child (Ruble et al., 2010). In this way, the team takes the focus off of the state standard as being the end goal, and instead puts the focus on the student's progress as the most important factor.

Similar to deficits in goal writing, a lack of identified accommodations also impacts an IEP's effectiveness. Without a set of clearly delineated accommodations and modifications, educators must guess at the most appropriate supports for a particular student (Ruble et al., 2010; Szidon, Ruppar, & Smith, 2015). When teams include generic accommodations that can be applied to all students, they have failed to create an individualized document. Many accommodations, especially those that assist with academic intervention (e.g., graphic organizers, pencil grips, calculation devices, etc.), can be generalized to fit many students with ASD; however, accommodations that are specific to social and functional communication and transition goals are often overlooked (Szidon, Ruppar, & Smith, 2015; Test, Smith, & Carter, 2014).

Teams may feel as though they are unable to provide specific accommodations to students due to a lack of resources available or lack of training opportunities on how to implement more intense accommodations, such as assistive technology and augmentative communication devices. Overall, support for team members in their execution of accommodations and modifications is a critical need for developing more effective IEPs and, subsequently, better educational planning for students with ASD (Ruble et al., 2010).

Exclusion Factors

For students with ASD, the most significant predictor of future success in education, employment, and independent living has been identified as inclusion in general education (Test, Smith, & Carter, 2014). Less than half of the total population of students ages 6 to 21 who have been diagnosed with ASD spend their day in a full-inclusion classroom (U.S. Department of Education, Office of Special Education and Rehabilitative Services, Office of Special Education Programs, 2015). Students with ASD who are excluded from their peers during the school day are less likely to participate in postsecondary education and more likely to experience negative adult outcomes (Chiang et al., 2012).

When students with ASD are included in the same classes as their typically developed peers, educators who are inexperienced in teaching students with ASD can inadvertently exclude these students through ineffective instructional practices which can ultimately affect students' access to the types of courses that would encourage them to pursue postsecondary educational opportunities (Test, Smith, & Carter, 2014).

Some students who have more intense needs, yet are included in general education classes, often find that comes at the cost of social interaction and academic engagement. Paraprofessionals are often assigned to individual students as a way of providing continual support throughout the school day. According to Test, Smith, and Carter (2014), there are over 430,000 paraprofessionals working with school-aged children who receive special education services.

While paraprofessional support can certainly help students with ASD to access the curriculum and utilize accommodations, their assistance can sometimes pose challenges to the academic and social advancement of students with ASD (Azad et al., 2015; Test, Smith, & Carter, 2014).

Many one-to-one assistants, for example, have been utilized incorrectly by the teachers with whom they work. Azad et al. (2015) cite studies in which one-to-one assistants have reported designing their own lesson plans, making determinations about appropriate behavioral approaches, and speaking with related service providers in order to establish appropriate classroom strategies. This suggests that there are many students with ASD who may miss out on instruction delivered by content-qualified professionals.

With regard to social skills development, students with ASD who are supported by a one-to-one paraprofessional are often segregated from their peers (Test, Smith, & Carter, 2014). The paraprofessional will often work with the student individually in another part of the room or in a separate space. This limits the amount of time the student has for exposure to social interactions with typically developed peers.

While many students with ASD receive myriad supports in order to help them move through their academic program, schools often lack the supports that would allow students to gain employment and postsecondary living skills. Studies suggest that employment outcomes for young adults with ASD are poor, and this is due in part to inadequate transition supports, including evidence-based instructional practices that focus on employment skills (Szidon, Ruppar, & Smith, 2015; Test, Smith, & Carter, 2014).

The lack of transition activities available to students with ASD creates an opportunity for these students to be excluded from the same types of opportunities as their typically developed peers (Test, Smith, & Carter, 2014). Schools may fail to effectively assess autistic students in the areas of career choice, postsecondary education, and independent living skills. This creates a missed opportunity for helping the student to plan an appropriate program of study.

Parental expectations have also been shown to have a direct impact on the choices available to students with ASD (Test, Smith, & Carter, 2014). When schools and parents fail to work together on behalf of the student, postsecondary choices become limited. Educators who have low expectations for students coupled with parents who are unaware of the potential postsecondary opportunities available to their child creates the perfect storm for a student to fall through the cracks (Chiang et al., 2012). Schools must do better to prevent that from happening.

TURNING CHALLENGES INTO SOLUTIONS

IEP Development

It is clear that a lack of teacher training, inappropriate assessments, poorly written IEPs, and exclusionary practices all negatively affect autistic students' abilities to achieve in a similar manner to their typically developed peers. Yet there are ways to make improvements through simple adjustments to practice. In 2014, the North Dakota Department of Public Instruction released a report detailing guidelines for serving students with ASD in the educational setting (North Dakota Department of Public Instruction, 2014). Within the report, educators were tasked with preparing students with ASD in key areas to include

- participate effectively in a learning group;
- use unstructured time wisely;

- self-regulate emotions and behavior;
- complete a work schedule;
- complete a learning schedule;
- complete work independently using visual supports or other necessary accommodations;
- get and keep a job;
- go on to higher education if desired; and
- pursue a vocational or technical career. (p. 6)

Having a clear understanding regarding the skills included in academic areas and in the domains of social interaction, communication, and adult living can help educators develop well-rounded plans that address the most critical areas of need for the student (Szidon, Ruppar, & Smith, 2015).

Knowing what needs to be done and actually bringing it to fruition are two separate challenges. The logical first step in creating effective educational programming for students with ASD begins with the development of the IEP. As previously stated, the IDEA (2006) outlines five specific domains that must be included in each IEP. Beginning with the student's present levels of performance, teams must consider where the student is currently functioning academically, developmentally, socially, and emotionally (Organization for Autism Research, 2012).

Without a clear statement of the student's current levels of performance, the team cannot go on to determine which aspects of ASD are having the biggest impact on the student's success or weaknesses in school. In addition to how the student is performing in school, the team must also include the most recent evaluation results and the parents' vision for student success. Having relevant data is critical in supporting decisions surrounding supports and interventions (Ruble et al., 2010).

Perhaps the most important step toward creating an effective education plan for a student with ASD is writing quality measurable goals. In their study on IEP evaluation tools, Ruble et al. (2010) found that goal writing was one of the greatest areas of need for improvement. One way to ensure that teams are writing effective goals is to consider the SMART goal method (Wright & Wright, 2008). SMART is an acronym for specific, measurable, action oriented, realistic and relevant, and time limited. Goals should be written in an unambiguous way that comprehensively cover the area of need and explain how progress will be measured (Organization for Autism Research, 2012; Szidon, Ruppar, & Smith, 2015; Wright & Wright, 2008).

Szidon, Ruppar, and Smith (2015) cite samples of ineffective goals surrounding transition planning; for example, "Chris will continue to take a study hall to allow for time during the school day to complete work and to maintain his study and organizational skills." In this goal, the reader can see that the goal is to help Chris improve his organizational skills; however, by merely stating he is going to take a study hall, Chris's progress is not being measured by how often he is completing homework or turning it in to his teachers. Furthermore, goals like this example show the ways in which goals can be met through passive participation (Chris's involvement in study hall) instead of actually measuring the real purpose of the goal (to increase Chris's organizational skills).

In order to effectively address the areas of ASD that are impacting the student the most, teams must often think outside the box to find ways that goals and objectives can be connected back to progress on standards. For example, the Organization on Autism Research (2012) suggests an exemplary goal might be that

> Jess will read one assigned paragraph at a 5th grade reading level (aloud) and will answer 10 questions (aloud or on paper) to measure comprehension of the material each week. By the end of the 2nd month of school, Jess will answer at least 60% correct, 70% by the 4th month, and 80% by the 6th month. If Jess is not making progress, she will be given the material to read in a different format or will use the help of a tutor. (p. 68)

In this example, the goal is specific to the student's need (reading comprehension at the fifth-grade level). It is also measurable (the student will read one paragraph and answer ten questions). The goal provides active words indicating what the student will be doing to achieve the goal ("will read," "will answer," "will use the help of a tutor").

The goal is relevant and realistic to the student's needs (making progress on reading comprehension will not only move the student closer to the state standard but also is a life skill that the student will need for successful postsecondary transition). Finally, the goal sets a time limit for progress (second month of school equals 60% correct, fourth month of school equals 70% correct, sixth month of school equals 80% correct). Although the IDEA specifies minimum requirements for what must be included in an IEP, states also have the freedom to require other information at their own discretion (Ruble et al., 2010).

Though IEPs can vary in format from state to state, it is crucial that the foundation remains the same. While the two previously mentioned examples are basic samples of both strong and weak goals, team members must remember that goals will look very different depending upon the need of the student. Some students may need much more narrow, targeted goals in order to achieve a particular skill (e.g., the student needs to learn basic math calculation skills beginning with addition), while others may need broader goals that aim to examine progress on a more overarching skill (e.g., the student needs to learn how to successfully initiate conversation with an unfamiliar person).

One last point on the topic of IEP development that is necessary to mention involves placement decisions for students with ASD. Placement recommendations are generally made by the team and should be dependent upon the student's need for support, not solely on the category of disability (Ruble et al., 2010). Many students are placed into special education programs based on their diagnoses; however, students with ASD may not need special education services to experience success in school and beyond (Test, Smith, & Carter, 2014).

It is up to the team to carefully consider the needs of each individual child in order to formulate the best plan. In accordance with least restrictive environment (LRE) mandates, students with disabilities must be educated alongside their nondisabled peers to the maximum extent appropriate (IDEA, 2006). Placement decisions must also be considered in accordance with the child's ability to make progress in a particular environment with the satisfactory use of supplementary aids and services (IDEA, 2006).

If placement cannot be achieved in a reasonable manner, other more restrictive placement options may be considered. Yet Ruble et al. (2010) state that the research suggests there is an overwhelming majority of placement decisions made without full consideration given to the student's complete profile, and it is decisions such as these that end up in litigation, costing school districts hundreds of thousands of dollars in legal fees (McKenney, 2017; Ruble et al., 2010).

Classroom Accommodations and Curriculum Modifications for Social and Communication Skills

For students with ASD, it is most often social and communication skills that are the most challenging factors when it comes to experiencing success in both school and society (Koegel et al., 2012; Test, Smith, & Carter, 2014). In order to help students with ASD develop the skills they need to function in societal situations, educators and service providers must carefully determine the most effective accommodations and modifications to curriculum. To do this, educators must first consider student learning styles (Celli & Young, 2014). All students have a preference for either visual, auditory, and/or kinesthetic, and it is up to the educators and plan creators to find the right mix of accommodations and modifications to address social, communication, and academic skills as needed (Celli & Young, 2014; Autism Speaks, 2012).

Communication Supports

Receptive and expressive language is an area in which students with ASD struggle; therefore, ensuring supports in the classroom are in place that address these areas of need are critical in maintaining the student's engagement. Suggested supports, dependent upon student need, that may be helpful for educators to employ include the following:

- Be sure to obtain the student's full attention before giving directions or asking questions.
- Provide the student with short, sequential steps to task completion.
- Use positive language when giving a direction (e.g., instead of using "don't walk" say, "walk on the sidewalk"). This limits potentially ambiguous words creating a clearer picture for the student to know exactly what is being directed.
- Allow the student to process information before asking for an answer or repeating the question.
- Use visual examples in addition to auditory commands.
- If the student has word retrieval difficulties, teach him or her to use picture cards or scripted phrases to help encourage reciprocal communication.
- Teach the student how to use augmentative communication devices.
- Utilize music, especially singing, in teaching new skills.
- Teach the student that emotions can be used for communication and help him or her to understand the appropriate ways in which to express emotions (e.g., teach the student that instead of hitting someone to show frustration, use a picture cue or visual to indicate the emotion that the student is feeling).
- As always, utilize positive reinforcement when a student performs a skill correctly, but refrain from negative language when a student performs a skill incorrectly. Instead, use encouraging words (e.g., "I like the effort you put into that assignment. Let's try these problems again"). (Autism Speaks, 2012)

Social Skills Supports

A common misunderstanding about children with ASD is that their lack of social reciprocity indicates their disinterest in engaging in social situations; however, that may not always be the case. Students with ASD often have the desire to engage with their peers yet have no skills that will allow them to interact appropriately (Autism Speaks, 2012; Koegel et al., 2012). Students with ASD may be very aware of their social deficits, which in turn leads them to avoid social situations at all costs. In order to encourage the ability for students with ASD to integrate into the population with their typically developed peers, educators should incorporate social-skill building into the day (Koegel et al., 2012; Ruble et al., 2010; Test, Smith, & Carter, 2014).

To accommodate students who need help with social-skill development, educators might try to do the following:

- Teach students to develop self-monitoring strategies through the use of a classroom cueing system or device designed to provide discreet reminders to the student.
- Use social stories in the classroom to help students with ASD develop an understanding of different perspectives as well as other people's feelings.
- Employ scaffolding of strategies within the classroom. Do not expect that the student will learn the best way to behave appropriately in a large group. Understand that small steps to integration may be the best way to help the student become comfortable in social situations.
- Do not engage the socially developing student in situations that require advanced flexible thinking (e.g., playing a game in which throwing a ball at students is acceptable, but not at adults).
- Model appropriate social interactions.
- Educate peers on the ways in which to become a supportive friend (Autism Speaks, 2012; Koegel et al., 2012).

Assessment Accommodations

More often than not, students with all categories of disability are required to participate in standardized testing; however, this can be especially challenging for students with ASD, even if they are academically functioning at grade level. Given the unique challenges associated with autism—communication, executive functioning, anxiety, social isolation—participating in standardized testing can prove next to impossible for autistic students.

Some of the more common accommodations provided on tests, for example, small group, calculation devices, extra time, and test read aloud, are often not enough to ultimately prove whether or not the student has mastered the content the exam is assessing (Bouck, 2013). Similarly, students with ASD who take and pass standardized exams are often seen as achieving success and may lose out on supports that are critically needed just because they can demonstrate a perceived ability to have mastered content (Bouck, 2013).

Standardized tests have a limited number of accommodations they will allow. In Massachusetts, the state standardized exam, the Massachusetts Comprehensive Assessment System (MCAS) has 40 standard accommodations that can be given to a student with a disability (Massachusetts Department of Elementary and Secondary Education, 2018). In order to qualify for any of the six additional nonstandard accommodations, students must meet specific criteria; for example, in order to qualify for a nonstandard accommodation such as spell checker for the English language arts (ELA) test, the student must "be virtually unable to spell simple words (i.e., at the beginning stages of learning how to spell), as documented by locally-administered diagnostic evaluations" (Massachusetts Department of Elementary and Secondary Education, 2018).

In the case of a student with ASD who may experience crippling test anxiety and would benefit from such an accommodation to take away the need to focus on spelling in favor of focusing on the content and structure of a written essay, this accommodation would not be allowed. While standardized assessments are not likely to disappear from the educational landscape in the foreseeable future, educators can keep in mind that students with ASD present with unique challenges that cannot easily be helped using standard accommodations.

Koegel et al. (2012) suggest that special attention should be paid to the attention given to the student prior to the assessment, the environment in which the assessment is conducted (individually, small group, or separate location), and the test administrator proctoring the assessment (familiar versus unfamiliar). These are factors that can have a large impact upon the student's success on a standardized exam. Furthermore, support from family in helping to prepare the student for the exam is critical in creating a successful testing day for a student with ASD (Koegel et al., 2012).

FINAL THOUGHTS

Developing an educational plan that is both appropriate and rigorous for a student with ASD can be a major challenge for educators (Morrier, Hess, & Heflin, 2011; Ruble et al., 2010; Test, Smith, & Carter, 2014). Taking the time to understand the ways in which students with ASD differ from students with other types of disabilities can help teachers, service providers, and other team members to design an educational plan that is in line with each student's needs. Continued professional development opportunities are needed to help teachers learn the best research-based practices and the ways in which to incorporate them into their classroom and curriculum (Anglim, Prendeville, & Kinsella, 2017; Boardman et al., 2005; Szidon, Ruppar, & Smith, 2015).

Educators must also not forget that ASD is a disability that affects much more than academic progress. In many cases, students with ASD are overlooked as to their need for social, communication, and executive functioning skill development (Autism Speaks, 2012; Kuo, 2016; Ruble & McGrew, 2013). When developing IEPs or making placement decisions, careful consideration must be made as to the student's current level of functioning as well as to the supports the student may need to make progress toward skill development (Ruble et al., 2010). Without all of the proper pieces to the puzzle in place, students with ASD are likely to fall through the cracks, experiencing poor outcomes in postsecondary life (Szidon, Ruppar, & Smith, 2015; Test, Smith, & Carter, 2014).

POINTS TO REMEMBER

- *One of the obstacles to providing FAPE to students with ASD is a misunderstanding of the ways in which to create effective educational programming (Anglim, Prendeville, & Kinsella, 2017; Morrier, Hess, & Heflin, 2011; Ruble et al., 2010; Ruble & McGrew, 2013).*
- *Teachers need ongoing training to ensure that they understand and are willing to use research-based interventions to improve the outcomes of autistic students (Koegel et al., 2012; Morrier, Hess, & Heflin, 2011).*
- *Effectively assessing students with ASD is a mix of multiple assessment types, not limited to standardized testing. The more opportunities to collect data, the more solidly developed the educational plan (Koegel et al., 2012).*
- *Goal writing is the biggest challenge for team members creating IEPs. Teams must remember that goals must be measurable and relevant to the individual student.*
- *Exclusionary practices are still an obstacle to the success of students with ASD.*
- *IEP teams must consider the unique challenges for students with ASD, including social, communication, and executive functioning skill deficits.*

Chapter Five

Helping Students with Autism Find Success in the Classroom

Promising Interventions

Extensive research has been conducted and has identified many evidence-based practices that are promising for students with autism (Council for Exceptional Children, 2014; Graham, Harris, & Chambers, 2016; Institute of Education Sciences, 2015). Evidence-based or research-based practices are strategies that have been proven effective through methodologically sound research studies.

Evidence-based practices, interventions, and/or strategies must be supported by strong evidence and credible research, which demonstrate positive student outcomes and are specific to an applicable academic, behavioral, or social domain, such as autism (Cook et al., 2008; Council for Exceptional Children, 2014). Implementation of evidence-based practices has been consistently shown to increase positive outcomes for students with disabilities, including autism. In addition, the use of evidence-based strategies is mandated by federal regulations including the Individuals with Disabilities Education Act (IDEA) of 2004 and the Every Student Succeeds Act (ESSA) of 2015 (Lee, 2018; Klein, 2016).

QUALIFYING AS AN EVIDENCE-BASED PRACTICE

The Council for Exceptional Children (CEC) is one agency that has released evidence-based practice standards including quality indicators that clearly define the criteria for identification of evidence-based practices (Council for Exceptional Children, 2014). The classifications include evidence-based practices, potentially evidence-based practices, having mixed effects, having negative effects, and having insufficient evidence to categorize their effectiveness (Council for Exceptional Children, 2014). In addition to the classifications, eight quality indicators were also identified and used to support the categorization. These quality indicators include context and setting, participants, intervention agent, description of practice, implementation fidelity, internal validity, outcome measures and dependent variables, and data analysis (Council for Exceptional Children, 2014). Having access to a set of standards ensures that teachers and service providers are able to choose the most highly effective strategies for their students.

In addition to the CEC standards, the Institute of Education Sciences: What Works Clearinghouse (2015) established rating criteria to determine the effectiveness of instructional strategies and interventions. Under these standards, the identification criterion assigns strategies or interventions into categories that include positive effects, potentially positive effects, mixed effects, potentially negative effects, negative effects, and no discernible effects (Kratochwill et al., 2013; Institute of Education Sciences: What Works Clearinghouse, n.d.). Having two governmental agencies develop similar standards for defining and labeling the level of proficiency of evidence-based practices ensures the continued effectiveness and use of these promising practices.

COMPONENTS OF EFFECTIVE EDUCATIONAL PLANNING FOR STUDENTS WITH AUTISM

Dunlap et al. (2010) examined the essential components for effective educational programming for students with autism. The authors claim that this population of students creates the greatest challenge for educators due to the spectrum of behavioral, academic, and social needs; thus, the desire to provide the most appropriate and effective instructional strategies is critical to creating optimal learning environments (Dunlap et al., 2010; Luiselli et al., 2008).

Before examining the essential components of educational programming for students with autism, it is helpful to look at 12 educational practices critical to working with the autistic student:

1. Carefully planning instruction, taking into consideration the characteristics present in those students with autism.
2. Ensuring efficient management of instructional time and creating structure and consistency, which are critical components.

3. The effective management of student behavior through well-planned classroom strategies to include the use of behavior plans, providing structure, and reinforcements.
4. Intentionally designing instructional groups to meet the learning needs of students and ensuring that students are paired with those with similar needs or with peer models. This has been proven effective through extensive research.
5. Considering the presentation of instructional stimuli and strategies ensures that students are engaged and focused on the lesson.
6. The establishment of structured classroom routines supports effective classroom management, thus creating an optimal learning environment.
7. It is necessary to provide students with frequent feedback that support the learning process, as this allows corrections to be made and confidence to be built.
8. Consistently monitoring student progress goes hand in hand with providing feedback.
9. Educators must engage in consistent review and reteaching of previously learned concepts to ensure mastery. This contributes to a solid foundation to build upon.
10. Integrating college and career readiness skills into the learning, such as critical thinking and problem-solving skills, teaches students to become successful in a variety of environments.
11. Setting appropriate expectations for all students based upon their individual needs creates attainable yet challenging opportunities for students to succeed.
12. Creating opportunities for positive interactions with peers and other adults offer ways to increase socialization skills (Westling, Fox, & Carter, 2014).

Examining the components of effective educational programming for students with autism reveals six critical aspects that must be considered in order to provide opportunities for success. These components take into consideration the communication and social deficits of students with autism and work to support these areas (Dunlap et al., 2010; Luiselli et al., 2008).

The first component, systematic instruction, implies that meaningful goals are developed and paired with explicit instruction to support said goals, creating opportunities for students to succeed in achieving their goals. Within this first component, data collection and progress monitoring are critical aspects. Collecting data and tracking progress toward goals determines if the student is progressing as expected or if the instructional technique is appropriate or if something different needs to be attempted (Dunlap et al., 2010; Zager, Wehmeyer, & Simpson, 2012).

The second component focuses on providing individualized supports and services. The best approach for this according to Dunlap et al. (2010) is to integrate research-based strategies found to support a broader range of characteristics. It is critical that supports and services are appropriately individualized according to the unique needs of each student. Further, when implementing strategies, the authors suggest that schools take into consideration the preferences of the family, the student's interests, and the strengths of the student in order to increase student achievement (Dunlap et al. 2010; Zager, Wehmeyer, & Simpson, 2012).

The third component is a logical and structured learning environment. Within this component, a structured learning environment is one where expectations are clearly defined and understandable to both the students and the staff (Dunlap et al., 2010; Luiselli et al., 2008). Further, the learning environment should be created and arranged to support, enhance, and enable the development of essential skills such as communication, socialization, behavioral, and of course academics (Dunlap et al., 2010).

The fourth component, a specialized curriculum focus, should place emphasis on the areas of deficits for students with autism, including communication and socialization (Dunlap et al., 2010). When the goal is to increase and support socialization, curriculum should focus on developing skills such as engaging in social situations, initiating and responding to social communication, comprehending social language, and appropriate participation in social events. Dunlap et al. (2010) recommend several approaches to teaching social skills for students with autism including naturalistic approaches, visual methods (such as social stories, video modeling), and through peer supports.

Supporting the communication needs of students with ASD should be based upon the principles of applied behavior analysis (ABA), according to Dunlap et al. (2010), including the use of discrete trials and fading prompts. The research also highlights the use of augmentative communication and assistive technology to increase communication (Zager, Wehmeyer, & Simpson, 2012). One extensively researched option would be the use of Picture Exchange Communication System (PECS), which uses the principles of ABA to increase communication by teaching students to exchange visual symbols (pictures) to request an object (National Autism Resources, 2018). With increased use and exposure, students can build up to using PECS to communicate in sentences and engage in reciprocal interactions (National Autism Resources, 2018; Zager, Wehmeyer, & Simpson, 2012).

The fifth component, providing a functional approach to dealing with problem behaviors, refers to implementing positive and proactive behavioral strategies based upon functional assessment data. This approach is known as positive behavioral support and is based in ABA theory and principles (Dunlap et al., 2010; Luiselli et al., 2008).

Positive behavioral supports begin with information from data collected through a functional behavioral assessment (FBA). An FBA provides information relative to the individual's function of his or her behavior. From this understanding, service providers are able to establish behavior plans that identify goals, supports, and strategies for changing the problematic behavior to a more desirable behavior (Zager, Wehmeyer, & Simpson, 2012).

The sixth component, family involvement, can be the most challenging; however, research has shown positive outcomes when increased levels of family involvement are provided. Improved student achievement, increased generalization of skills, and higher school program acceptance rates by families are prevalent in the research as gains that can be made (Dunlap et al., 2010; Luiselli et al., 2008).

Several strategies are highlighted as effective for enhancing family involvement in the education of students with autism. The first strategy includes teaching families how to implement interventions, while providing training to families around improving interactions during unstructured times at home has proved helpful. Finally, explaining the purpose and facilitation of positive behavioral supports to use in the home setting is imperative for family buy-in and student success (Dunlap et al., 2010; Luiselli et al., 2008; Zager, Wehmeyer, & Simpson, 2012).

PROMISING EVIDENCE-BASED INTERVENTIONS FOR STUDENTS WITH AUTISM

Social Skills Development

Social skills are tremendously important for individuals with ASD to develop, but also incredibly difficult to learn (Thompson, 2017). The most important social skills are eye contact, the ability to request, the ability to imitate, displaying low levels of inappropriate behavior, and the ability to play with toys appropriately (Wilkinson, 2014). The learning of these early social skills should include assistance through discrete trial training (DTT) and modeling.

It is important to explain to students the idea of compromising to promote positive social skills development, and one way to do this is visual sequencing (Wilkinson, 2014). You can show the child a picture of two children playing, compromising, and smiling. Then, you can show the opposite, children playing, not compromising, with sad faces. What follows is a sampling of promising practices and curriculums for increasing social skills and academic skills for autistic students.

Video Modeling

One proven method to teach children with autism social and play skills is through video modeling:

> Video modeling and computer instruction interventions have usually involved taping a short video sequence of the child with autism, a typically developing peer, or an adult performing the target social skills and then showing this video to the child before social opportunities. (Luiselli et al., 2008, p. 289)

Weiss (2007) states that "many students with ASD are strong visual learners, and many enjoy watching videos. They may attend better to a model presented in a video clip than they would to a live model demonstrating a skill" (p. 25).

Videos that support the upcoming situation should be shown to the student before they will be in an unfamiliar environment (Wilkinson, 2014). There are several benefits to using video modeling including that the videos are typically short, which keeps the student focused, they can be used several times to help reinforce the skills learned, the videos can be paused at any time to further explain a piece of the video, and they are also showing real-life situations to help with generalization (Luiselli et al., 2008; Weiss, 2007; Zager, Wehmeyer, & Simpson, 2012).

A curriculum called Model Me Kids provides evidence-based videos for modeling social skills. Modeling peer behavior in natural environments helps students with ASD understand how to build and use their personal social skills repertoire. The program includes videos, apps, software, teaching manuals, and student workbooks (Model Me Kids, 2017).

Peer-Mediated Interventions

Peer-mediated interventions are a proven, evidenced-based method of teaching social skills for children with autism (Wilkinson, 2014). The method of using typically developing peers that have been trained to work as buddies and/or tutors with their classmates "allows for facilitation of social skills" (Luiselli et al., 2008, p. 286). Peer-mediated intervention may involve working one-on-one with a student or with a group of students and, in some cases, an entire class.

Peer-mediated teaching within the age group of three to eight encourages typical peers and the autistic student to learn play skills, sharing, and so forth, and this fosters the development of their communication, language, and social skills (Wilkinson, 2014). For older students, ages 9 to 18, the peer-mediated teaching focuses more on the social component of interactions between typically developing peers and their autistic classmates by implementing more social opportunities for learning and also fosters a "higher acceptance and tolerance for human differences" (Luiselli et al., 2008, p. 287).

Social Stories

Social stories are used to increase a student's awareness and understanding of social situations that the student may encounter. Social stories were developed in the early 1990s as a way to "address a variety of target skills, most commonly conversation skills, play skills, and pivotal behaviors" (Luiselli et al., 2008, p. 279). With the development of social stories, significant social skill deficits can be addressed for children with autism. "Beginning with the child's understanding of a situation, a story is developed describing what is happening and why, and how people feel and think in the situation. While the story contains some directive statements, the focus is on understanding what is happening in the situation" (Baker, 2005, p. 19).

According to Austin (2011), social stories are easy to develop and implement in classrooms. Social stories give objective information about a variety of social situations to provide the students with social cues and correct responses (Gray, 2015). They also help break down a complex scenario into smaller steps. This method has been used to aid in transitions, new activities, daily routines, challenging behaviors, personal hygiene, and classroom expectations (Austin, 2011). Social stories should be read prior to an activity in order to be the most useful and read consistently at the same place and time (Gray, 2015).

When developing a social story, it is important to keep four components in mind. First, the use of descriptive sentences—the who, what, where, when, and why of the story—should be used to describe a social setting or to provide sequential steps for completing an activity (Gray, 2015). Second, the use of perspective sentences as a way to reflect another's perspective. Third, incorporation of directive sentences; these should begin with "I will work on . . ." or "I will try . . ." describing the responses the person should ideally make (Gray, 2015). Fourth, providing control sentences that describe strategies that can help the individual remember the information presented within the story (Gray, 2015).

There are several preplanning steps that need to be addressed before creating a social story. The target behavior should be identified by gathering information from the IEP and direct observations (Austin, 2011). It is also important to identify all of the "wh-" questions surrounding the social situation. The function of the behavior or what you believe the student is attempting to communicate through the behavior must be included as a final step prior to writing the social story (Austin, 2011).

Social stories should be short and to the point and should grab the student's attention and align with the student's reading ability (Gray, 2015).

Social stories should be personalized to each student and should be written using first-person perspectives and incorporate the use of positive language (Austin, 2011; Gray, 2015). Social stories should be read frequently throughout the day and may be incorporated into the student's daily binder, during instructional time, or during morning meeting (Long, 2018). It is also important to choose only one goal to teach and practice at a time (Long, 2018).

Priming

In addition to social stories, priming is another intervention you can use to teach students appropriate social skills. "Priming is a type of antecedent intervention in which the target behavior is practiced immediately before being performed. Priming sessions consist of verbal modeling and instruction to perform a behavior, followed by reinforcement of that behavior" (Luiselli et al., 2008, p. 280).

Antecedent strategies such as priming have been effective in helping individuals with autism to learn social skills. Priming helps to teach a social skill and prepares the individual to exhibit appropriate behavior in the setting where it will be needed. Using multiple examples can help to promote generalization among autistic students. Baker (2005) notes that teachers have to explicitly plan to teach skills that do not come naturally and to encourage their students to generalize those skills to other settings.

One method, called Identiplay, incorporates the use of scripts to teach social skills as a way to build rapport and relationships, imitation, gaining attention, turn taking, enjoyment, and structure (Phillips & Beavan, 2012). Identiplay has two key guidelines that consist of the use of simple narrative structures and the teacher leading the play (Phillips & Beavan, 2012). The method uses a table that is split into two sections with chairs facing each other across the table and identical toys on either side.

Using a script and specific scenario, the teacher leads the play with each toy and the child is expected to model or imitate them, giving the child a chance to learn to engage and reply to appropriate play by teaching through modeling and imitation (Phillips & Beavan, 2012). Similar to the method of social stories, Identiplay offers more options with hands-on manipulatives and active participation, which is slightly more complex (Phillips & Beavan, 2012).

Pictures and/or visual scripts provide another way to assist with skills development and task completion (Weiss, 2007). Picture scripts are step-by-step picture directions that use student motivations and interests, current skill level, and the teacher's help to implement (Weiss, 2007). Picture scripts can be used to help teach children with autism new communication and play skills (Harris et al., 2013). Picture scripts can help children with ASD carry out the steps of an activity with little support or adult modeling as well as increase independence and communication skills (Harris et al., 2013).

THE SOCIAL SKILLS INTERVENTION GUIDE

The *Social Skills Intervention Guide* is an evidence-based PK–12 social skills guide that offers 20 instructional units with resources that support instruction and tools to monitor progress (Elliot & Gresham, 2008). The curriculum covers seven social skill domains including communication, cooperation, assertion, responsibility, empathy, engagement, and self-control and includes a step-by step teaching model based on these domains (Elliot & Gresham, 2008). The guide gives practical tips for grouping students, involving parents, and creating goals for the students. The main focus is geared toward students receiving tier II interventions within a response to intervention (RTI) framework.

The program focuses on skills that do not come naturally as well as how to promote generalization of skills through case studies, sample lessons, examples, and activities (Elliot & Gresham, 2008). The *Social Skills Intervention Guide* involves the use of role playing and gives guidelines on how to use reinforcement strategies in conjunction with the guide. Weiss (2007) claims that data collected on the effectiveness of all strategies implemented with individual learners is critical to achieving results. The *Social Skills Intervention Guide* curriculum monitors student progress while classifying deficits in social skill areas (Elliot & Gresham, 2008).

Adolescent Curriculum for Communication and Effective Social Skills

The Walker Social Skills Curriculum: *The ACCESS Program, Adolescent Curriculum for Communication and Effective Social Skills* is a curriculum for teaching effective social skills to students in middle and high school (Walker et al., 1987). It teaches peer-to-peer interaction skills, skills for relating to adults, and self-management techniques. Unlike the *Social Skills Intervention Guide*, the ACCESS program can be taught in one-to-one settings along with group settings.

The program contains 30 different social story scripts for teachers to follow for students in middle and high school as well as a student study guide that contains role-playing scripts and discrimination exercises (Walker et al., 1987). Similar to the *Social Skills Intervention Guide*, it offers suggestions on grouping students and also gives tips such as how to motivate, manage behaviors, and how to make sure generalization occurs (Walker et al., 1987).

Learn to Play Therapy

Luiselli et al. (2008) state that "learning how to appropriately manipulate toys is an important prerequisite skill for game play and cooperative play with other children" (p. 276). A program that works on this skill helps children build their spontaneous play ability (Stagnitti, 2018). The play skills focused on in Learn to Play Therapy include the ability to spontaneously self-initiate play, sequencing play actions logically, object substitution or symbols in play, integrating play so a clear play script is evident, role play, and socially interacting using play (Stagnitti, 2018).

Symbolic and imaginative play developmental checklists are used in this therapy to monitor progress and growth. Principles in this type of therapy include starting where the child's play ability is, emotionally engaging the child in the play activity, being aware of the play script, the number of actions in a play sequence, the use of symbols in play, and challenging the child when you think the child is ready, working toward the child taking over the play, always responding to the child, and always monitoring that the play is coherent (Stagnitti, 2018).

We Thinkers! Social Explorers Curriculum

This curriculum consists of five books that help to teach thoughts and feelings, thinking with your eyes, following the group plan, keeping your body in the group, and whole body listening (Social Thinking, 2018). The books incorporate four characters, Jessie, Molly, Evan, and Ellie, and the four of them go on adventures and teach each other how to be friends and work together as a team to complete a task (Social Thinking, 2018).

Baker (2005) talks about generalization and being able to use a newly learned skill in the natural environment. Because this curriculum is implemented in a small group, the students are learning these skills in their natural environment and hopefully this will make generalizing the skills throughout the school day easier for them (Baker, 2005).

Circle Curriculum

In order to teach social boundaries, the use of the Circle Curriculum is an effective approach. This curriculum is a visual and interactive way to teach children about how to interact with various people within their environments from strangers to friends, all the way down to themselves (Stanfield, 2018). It is an outstanding way to educate about stranger danger, safety, and personal space for children who may not find these topics intuitive (Stanfield, 2018). Not only does it offer visual models but it also strives to explain how relationships and intimacy levels can change over time and offers real-life models to help children recognize situations and react appropriately.

Hidden Curriculum

The Hidden Curriculum is derived from the concept that when we are teaching any kind of lesson there are unintended things that we are also communicating to our students (Alsubaie, 2015). Hidden Curriculum looks at social situations that neurotypical individuals tend to have a social intuition for, establishes what the unspoken rules of those situations are, and then expressly explains those rules. It addresses things such as slang and idioms as well as things like the rules of using a public restroom, going to the pool, or attending a birthday party (Alsubaie, 2015).

It may not be apparent to teachers that rules of these social situations need to be expressly taught because we often navigate them unconsciously. Having a curriculum that clearly details and explains these social situations can help teachers know which rules we need to ensure are explained in detail. The curriculum also includes visuals, such as charts, which greatly help assisting students in developing skills and supporting role playing situations (Alsubaie, 2015).

FINAL THOUGHTS

To be considered an evidence-based practice, an intervention or strategy must be proven to be effective by extensive research (Council for Exceptional Children, 2014; Graham, Harris, & Chambers, 2016; Institute of Education Sciences, 2015). Continuous research has proven the positive effects of evidence-based practices and achievement for students with disabilities (Graham, Harris, & Chambers, 2016; Institute of Education Sciences, 2015). In addition, under federal regulations, including the Individuals with Disabilities Education Act (2004) and the Every Student Succeeds Act (2015), the use of evidence-based practices are mandated.

Dunlap et al. (2010) discussed the educational practices that are critical to working with autistic students. The research also highlighted the necessary components of any program for educating and supporting autistic students as well as many evidence-based interventions, curriculums, and strategies (Dunlap et al., 2010; Luiselli et al., 2008; Zager, Wehmeyer, & Simpson, 2012).

POINTS TO REMEMBER

- *The use of evidence-based practices, as mandated by federal regulations, has been proven to be highly effective at closing the achievement gap and boosting student outcomes for those with disabilities.*

- *Evidence-based practices have been identified as effective through extensive and rigorous research studies and qualification standards.*
- *The literature has highlighted several components, critical to the success of any program developed to support autistic students to include the use of systematic instruction, providing individualized supports, creating and maintaining a comprehensible and structured learning environment, providing a specialized curriculum focus, providing a functional approach to behavior problems, and family involvement.*

Chapter Six

Applied Behavior Analysis and Effective Classroom Instruction

Strategies that Foster the Best in our Students

Individuals with ASD present with many unique characteristics that require the use of specialized teaching strategies. Applied behavior analysis (ABA) offers effective strategies for learners with autism because it is not just one way of thinking and educating students (Autism Speaks, 2018c). ABA is individualized, and there are multiple ways to use ABA principles to better understand behaviors and identify strategies to help change targeted behaviors to more desirable behaviors; thus, each student receives exactly what they need in order to find success (Webber & Scheuermann, 2008; Zager, Wehmeyer, & Simpson, 2012).

ABA incorporates data collection on any and all behaviors that inform educators on student abilities and needs. Data sheets are a simple and concrete way to interpret and understand student behaviors. It is only with this understanding that appropriate help can be given. ABA procedures are based on the concept that a behavior is the result of antecedents that precede it and the consequences that follow it (Autism Speaks, 2018c). Antecedents and consequences can be manipulated to increase the likelihood that desired behaviors will occur and undesired behaviors will be reduced or eliminated (Webber & Scheuermann, 2008).

ABA is often effective with students who have ASD because of the way behaviors are understood, targeted, and either encouraged or discouraged accordingly (Autism Speaks, 2018c). ABA is unique in that it can keep up with what might seem chaotic to more traditional forms of instruction; thus, therapies based on these principles may help.

APPLIED BEHAVIOR ANALYSIS

A significant approach in educating students on the spectrum is applied behavior analysis (ABA). It is one of the methods used to study behaviors in children with developmental delays and often, ASD. It is an intervention of sorts that collects data on behavior and environmental factors of those behaviors. The data is then analyzed and used to increase or decrease positive or negative behaviors, respectively (Zager, Wehmeyer, & Simpson, 2012).

ABA is a strategy backed by over 50 years of research and theory (Webber & Scheuermann, 2008). ABA is an evidence-based instructional strategy that supports behavior change and has been proven to produce desired outcomes for individuals with autism. ABA encompasses an array of assessments, interventions, and evaluation procedures that, when used in myriad combinations, can create individualized programs for individuals with ASD based upon their specific needs (Webber & Scheuermann, 2008; Zager, Wehmeyer, & Simpson, 2012).

ABA consists of instructional and behavioral principles that follow a simple ABC model: antecedents, behavior, and consequences (Luiselli et al., 2008; Webber & Scheuermann, 2008; Zager, Wehmeyer, & Simpson, 2012). Antecedents are the events that occur before, or just prior to, a behavior. The behavior demonstrated by the individual is the direct result of the antecedent. When analyzing behaviors, it is important to assess the antecedents to determine the level of influence on the behavior (Webber & Scheuermann, 2008; Zager, Wehmeyer, & Simpson, 2012).

Behaviors are essentially the center or target of any intervention within the ABA framework. Behaviors can include anything from language, motor, social, work or daily living, or self-help. When choosing a behavior to target, it is critical to clearly identify the specific behavior so that the most appropriate teaching intervention can be implemented (Webber & Scheuermann, 2008; Zager, Wehmeyer, & Simpson, 2012).

Clearly describing a behavior is referred to as an operational definition. It is a good rule of thumb to have two or more individuals operationalize the behavior to ensure an adequate description is used. As a result, proper and consistent interventions, progress measuring, and consequences can be provided and recorded (Luiselli et al., 2008; Webber & Scheuermann, 2008).

Consequences are given after a behavior has occurred. The consequence will determine if a behavior will likely occur again. There are several types of reinforcements including positive reinforcement, secondary reinforcements, and negative reinforcements. When the consequence is positive, meaning that the consequence is a desirable item or activity for the individual, it is likely that the behavior will occur again; whereas a consequence that is negative will negate the behavior over time (Webber & Scheuermann, 2008; Zager, Wehmeyer, & Simpson, 2012).

Positive reinforcement is a method of producing repeated desired behaviors through implementation of encouraging consequences. By rewarding the student with a meaningful consequence immediately following a desired behavior, the more likely the student is to engage in that behavior again (Luiselli et al., 2008; Webber & Scheuermann, 2008; Zager, Wehmeyer, & Simpson, 2012). Reinforcers are either primary/intrinsic such as food, or secondary/extrinsic, such as activities. Primary reinforcers are the most effective, especially with individuals with low cognition (Webber & Scheuermann, 2008).

Secondary reinforcers are things that the individual learns to like and fall into several categories: social, material, activity, or token. Social reinforcers refer to praise or acknowledgment. Material reinforcers relate to any object the student may show an interest in. An activity reinforcer might be such things as playing a game or video, while a token reinforcer includes a chip or token that can be saved and collected to be turned in at a later time for a desired reinforcement (Webber & Scheuermann, 2008; Zager, Wehmeyer, & Simpson, 2012).

Discrete Trial Training

Discrete trial training (DTT) is a lesson-presentation method based in the principles of ABA. Also known as trial-by-trial training or discrete trial format, this method is primarily used for teaching and drilling new responses and skills (Luiselli et al., 2008; Webber & Scheuermann, 2008). DTT consists of larger skills broken down into smaller, teachable steps. This is beneficial for children with ASD as they are more apt to have difficulty in being able to complete large skills or understand the complexity of that particular skill. Breaking down the steps will help the individual learn each specific step and then be able to put them all together.

Through DTT, the student receives assistance from the teacher or service provider in the form of cues, instructions, expectations, and feedback. This assistance allows students with ASD to make sense of their world (Webber & Scheuermann, 2008). Through the DTT process, students know what the expected response is, they receive assistance in responding, immediate feedback is given, and students receive a desired reinforcer (Luiselli et al., 2008; Webber & Scheuermann, 2008).

DTT is typically implemented in a distraction-free environment and is comprised of (1) a cue in the form of a verbal or nonverbal stimulus presentation; (2) a prompt, if needed, used to evoke a correct response; (3) the child's response; (4) a consequence/reinforcer, contingent on a child's response; and (5) an intertrial interval, wherein there is a brief pause before the next trial begins (Zager, Wehmeyer, & Simpson, 2012).

There are five components within a DTT session. The first component, discriminative stimulus, is the presentation of a stimulus to the student, also known as the antecedent. Within DTT, the antecedent would be the instruction given by the teacher. The instruction must be clear and very specific to the skill being taught (Webber & Sceuermann, 2008). It is important to note that within DTT, a discriminative stimulus is referred to as instruction that cues a certain desired behavior (Webber & Scheuermann, 2008; Zager, Wehmeyer, & Simpson, 2012).

When delivering discriminative stimulus within DTT, it is important to gain the full attention of the student prior. A teacher or service provider can gain attention through praise and prompting (Webber & Scheuermann, 2008). Once the student is attending, the teacher or service provider should present the instruction clearly and specifically, making sure the directions are simplified and ensuring that there is a clear beginning and end, as this assists the student in understanding what is expected (Luiselli et al., 2008; Webber & Scheuermann, 2008; Zager, Wehmeyer, & Simpson, 2012).

Further, when giving the instruction, it should be prominent and not competing with other environmental stimuli. In order to accomplish this, the teacher or service provider should speak louder, emphasize particular words, and even incorporate visuals (Webber & Scheuermann, 2008; Zager, Wehmeyer, & Simpson, 2012). In order to gain control of the stimulus, there must be consistency between service providers. This means that different providers must use the same wording, prompts, and cues, until the student has produced the desired skill or behavior with little to no assistance (Webber & Scheuermann, 2008).

The second component of DTT is prompting. A prompt is any form of assistance provided to the student to help him or her respond correctly to a direction (Zager, Wehmeyer, & Simpson, 2012). According to Webber and Scheuermann (2008), prompting is one of the most effective principles of DTT and other forms of direct instruction. There are several kinds of prompts including verbal, visual, and physical. Verbal prompts include any type of verbal instruction or hint given to the student. Visual prompts are anything that the student can see for assistance, such as a picture, video, gesture, object, or schedule. A physical prompt is any manual assistance provided to the student, such as the teacher putting his or her hand over a student's hand to show the student how to hold a pencil.

The third component of DTT includes the student response or targeted behavior. Before a student can respond, it is critical that the teacher or service provider know precisely what the behavior should be (Luiselli et al., 2008; Zager, Wehmeyer, & Simpson, 2012). The behavior must be operationally defined, meaning that it is clearly measurable and observable (Webber & Scheuermann, 2008). Within a DTT session, after the stimulus is presented, the student can either respond correctly, respond incorrectly, or not respond at all. It is imperative that an appropriate amount of wait-time is given for the student to respond—approximately 5 to 10 seconds—to facilitate a correct response. Some students may need some extra processing time to respond (Webber & Scheuermann, 2008; Zager, Wehmeyer, & Simpson, 2012).

The fourth component of DTT includes the consequence, which is the reaction of the teacher or service provider to the student's response (Webber & Scheuermann, 2008; Zager, Wehmeyer, & Simpson, 2012). Within DTT, only positive reinforcers should be provided. The goal of DTT is to introduce and practice new behaviors and skills, which we want the student to engage in again in the future.

The fifth and final component of DTT is known as intertrial interval, which refers to the amount of time between the student receiving a consequence and beginning a new trial (Webber & Scheuermann, 2008). Intertrial intervals allow for the distinction between trials, time for the teacher or service provider to record student responses, and opportunities to reward attending behaviors and build a bond with the student (Webber & Scheuermann, 2008; Zager, Wehmeyer, & Simpson, 2012).

This type of teaching is beneficial to students with ASD for several reasons including the following:

- The ease of implementation, which means that many teachers and service providers within the school setting can be trained on how to implement the program.
- Classroom implementation is preferred, which means that students would not have to be taken out of the classroom to engage in trials.
- Data can be easily collected during the trials to track how the students are progressing.
- Multiple practice opportunities can happen within a short amount of time.
- The instructions to complete the trial are clearly written to ensure that all educators use the same wording every time.

Additional program benefits include the completely individualized choice of trials based upon the student: from the discriminate stimulus, to the prompt (if any), to the consequence. In addition, each individual student may need to learn the same skills, yet the trials will be set up to fit the unique needs of each child, setting him or her up for success.

Data collection is facilitated. Since data collection and analysis are important to help the learner move from being taught to mastery, if data is not being collected, the student may never move on to the next target. Having the data collection built into the programs ensures consistency and ongoing analysis, which supports modification of the program if required (Webber & Scheuermann, 2008).

Errorless learning and prompting are part of DTT, both of which contribute to successful outcomes. Students with ASD who get the correct answer or exhibit the correct response with little or less effort are less likely to show challenging behaviors. Further, DTT incorporates intensive drill and practice opportunities (Webber & Scheuermann, 2008). DTT can be implemented anywhere by any person who is trained; thus, the student is exposed to more opportunities to be taught, leading to greater generalization of the skill.

Generalization is a critical part of DTT, as the student must be able to exhibit the newly mastered skill in different environments, with other people, and across time in order for it to be beneficial. Generalization can be incorporated into the personalized programs to ensure a plethora of opportunities occur that lead to complete mastery (Webber & Scheuermann, 2008; Zager, Wehmeyer, & Simpson, 2012).

Naturalistic and Milieu Teaching

Naturalistic teaching strategies are based in the principles of ABA and focus on developing communication and language skills (Webber & Scheuermann, 2008). Other common terms for naturalistic teaching are natural environment training, natural language paradigm, and incidental teaching; however, regardless of the name, this type of teaching takes advantage of the natural environment where students are naturally motivated to behave (Webber & Scheuermann, 2008; Zager, Wehmeyer, & Simpson, 2012). The stimuli within naturalistic teaching occur within the environment, and the teacher or service provider proactively creates opportunities for learning to occur through teachable moments.

According to Hart and Risley (1982), incidental teaching is when the natural environment is arranged to attract the child to desired materials and activities, and the teacher is available to provide attention, praise, and instruction when the child initiates interaction with materials. There are four procedures that support the practice of naturalistic teaching including modeling, mand-modeling, time delay, and environmental manipulation. For modeling to occur, the teacher or service provider must get to know the student well in order to discover the student's preferences and interests. Once this is established the teacher will model or demonstrate a functional behavior related to the student's desired interest (Webber & Scheuermann, 2008; Zager, Wehmeyer, & Simpson, 2012). For example, if a student is interested in completing a puzzle, the teacher may demonstrate how to look for a piece and fit it into the puzzle.

Mand-modeling includes the use of a mand or verbal instruction. Within naturalistic teaching, the environment is proactively set up to elicit desired student behaviors and provide ample opportunities to practice. Once a student shows interest in a certain activity, the teacher would gain the student's attention and provide verbal mands (requests) to produce the desired behavior. Verbal mands such as "use your words" or "tell me what you want" are common (Luiselli et al., 2008; Webber & Scheuermann, 2008; Zager, Wehmeyer, & Simpson, 2012).

The time-delay procedure is used when students know how to produce the desired behavior but are reluctant to do so or the student is practicing the skill within generalization contexts (Webber & Scheuermann, 2008). When using time delay, the teacher or service provider gains the student's attention once the student displays interest or distress. Once attention is gained, the teacher or service provider then waits 5 to 15 seconds for the student to engage in the desired behavior. Time delay is useful in fading out the amount of assistance provided to the student (Webber & Scheuermann, 2008) and therefore increasing independence.

The final component, environmental manipulation, is the basis for naturalistic teaching. Teachers and service providers should thoroughly assess their students to discover interests and what will motivate students to engage in desirable behaviors (Luiselli et al., 2008; Webber & Scheuermann, 2008; Zager, Wehmeyer, & Simpson, 2012). There are several ways that this can be accomplished, such as disrupting routines, disrupting compulsions, providing interesting materials, leaving things unfulfilled, placing things out of reach, providing choices, constructing barriers, and providing surprises (Webber & Scheuermann, 2008; Zager, Wehmeyer, & Simpson, 2012).

Similarities and Differences Between DTT and Incidental Teaching Methods

Research has shown that both DTT and incidental teaching methods are helpful at increasing expressive and receptive language skills. DTT provides short trials that allow for more learning opportunities throughout the day, while incidental teaching begins with the child's mand and a variety of language skills that can be taught. In both teaching methods, responses are related to identification of target responses and environmental arrangements (Fenske, Krantz, & McClannahan, 2001). Both strategies build language skills, use antecedents and prompts to evoke targeted responses, and use the principles of ABA (Fenske, Krantz, & McClannahan, 2001).

The most notable difference between the two strategies is that incidental teaching takes place in a more natural setting for the student, which helps identify motivators and reinforcers. Incidental teaching uses materials related to what is being taught, provides more opportunity for generalization to occur, and is initiated by the learner; whereas DTT typically teaches labeling and is initiated by the teacher (Jennett, Harris, & Delmolino, 2008).

These lists highlight the similarities and differences between the two most common strategies within ABA.

Incidental or Naturalistic Teaching

- students are naturally motivated to behave
- antecedent stimuli occur naturally
- begins with a child's initiation for materials, activity, or topic that is highly preferred
- done in a natural environment
- materials/rewards chosen by the child
- usually addresses mand training or requesting
- teaches play, self-help, and occupational skills

Discrete Trial Training (DTT)

- task is initiated by teacher or parent
- in a structured learning environment
- materials and rewards are chosen by instructor
- typically teaches tactile or labeling
- highly structured
- well established and used for teaching cognitive skills

Both Methods (Naturalistic and DTT)

- positive reinforcement
- break down of information to manageable chunks
- both based on ABA
- teach language, social skills, and academics

PIVOTAL RESPONSE TRAINING

Pivotal response training (PRT) helps to teach foundational skills needed before acquiring more complex skills (Jung & Sainato, 2013). In teaching play, for example, PRT is used in the natural environment while utilizing discrete trial methods. The teacher models appropriate play and then it is the child's turn. Appropriate play demonstrated by the child is reinforced and this then continues with a turn-taking process (Jung & Sainato, 2013). PRT incorporates generalization strategies such as "training loosely, teaching in criterion settings, teaching using multiple examples, and programming common stimuli between training and generation settings" (Luiselli et al., 2008, p. 288).

ADDITIONAL EVIDENCE-BASED PRACTICES FOR TEACHING STUDENTS WITH AUTISM

In addition to DTT and naturalistic training, a long list exists of promising evidence-based practices for teaching students who have ASD (Vanderbilt Peabody College, 2014).

Antecedent-based interventions include arranging events and circumstances that precede an interfering behavior. This leads to the reduction of the behavior occurring. In order to accurately change the antecedent, a functional behavior assessment helps to clarify the cause of the behavior and identify the specific antecedents.

Cognitive behavioral interventions include direct instruction related to managing or controlling the cognitive process of changing inappropriate behavior.

Differential reinforcement of alternative, incompatible, or other behavior (DRA, DRI, or DRO) includes providing a positive consequence or reinforcement for positive behavior or a lack of inappropriate behavior. DRA occurs when the reinforcement is given to the student when the student is engaged in desired behavior. DRI occurs when the reinforcement is given when the student is engaged in a behavior that is physically impossible to do when exhibiting the inappropriate behavior. DRO occurs when the reinforcement is given to the student when the student is not engaged in the appropriate behavior.

Extinction is the withdrawal or removal of a reinforcer in order to decrease inappropriate behaviors. Extinction can occur as a standalone intervention or can be used in conjunction with another appropriate approach.

Functional behavioral assessment is an approach in which information is collected about a problem behavior. The information collected is analyzed to identify the function of the behavior, including the antecedents and consequences.

Functional communication training encompasses replacing a behavior that has a communication function with more appropriate communication that accomplishes the same function. Functional communication training is usually combined with a functional behavior assessment, differential reinforcement, and/or extinction.

Modeling is the demonstration of a desired behavior by a teacher, service provider, or peer that results in the imitation of the behavior. Modeling is often used in conjunction with prompting and reinforcement.

Peer-mediated instruction engages typical peers to interact and provide assistance to those children with autism. These interactions help to develop appropriate communication, social, and behavioral skills. Peer-mediated instruction typically occurs in the natural environment.

Picture Exchange Communication System (PECS) is an intervention that uses visual representations to engage students in communication. There are six phases of PECS: how to communicate, distance and persistence, picture discrimination, sentence structure, responsive requesting, and commenting.

Pivotal response training (PRT) encompasses variables such as motivation, responding to multiple cues, self-management, and self-initiations, which guide the intervention to build upon the learner's skills and interests.

Prompting includes verbal and/or physical assistance provided to the student from a teacher or service provider in order for the student to engage in a targeted behavior or skill.

Reinforcements such as a desired event, activity, or item provided after a desired behavior occurs increases the chance that the behavior will continue in the future.

Scripting refers to a verbal or written description about a specific skill or situation that a student uses as a model. Scripting is usually practiced repeatedly until the student implements the skill in an actual situation.

Self-management includes the student individually discriminating between appropriate and inappropriate behaviors, monitoring and recording behaviors, and rewarding appropriate behaviors.

Social narratives describe social situations, providing details and cues, to highlight appropriate responses and behaviors. Social narratives, also referred to as social stories, are individualized based upon the student's needs. Social narratives can include pictures and visuals to support the story as well.

Social skills training is used to teach appropriate interactions with peers, adults, and other individuals. Social skills training can occur in groups or in an individual setting. Social skills training can include role playing, video modeling, and feedback to assist students in acquiring the skills needed to practice communication, play, and socialization to support positive interactions.

Task analysis is a process that takes a skill or activity and breaks it down into simple steps or manageable chunks in order for students to learn and practice the desired behavior. When using task analysis, reinforcements, video modeling, and time delay are usually used in conjunction as well.

Time delay is a strategy in which a brief delay occurs between an opportunity to use a skill and any additional instruction or prompt is provided. The purpose of time delay is to allow the learner to respond without additional help or support as a means of fading prompts.

Video modeling provides the student with a visual model of a targeted behavior or skill to assist in the learning or engagement in the behavior.

Visual supports include any visual that supports the learner in engaging in the desired behavior without the use of prompts. Visual supports include such things as pictures, written words, objects, maps, labels, organization systems, or timelines.

FINAL THOUGHTS

Applied behavior analysis (ABA) is backed by over 50 years of research (Luiselli et al., 2008; Zager, Wehmeyer, & Simpson, 2012). The theories and principles upon which ABA is built help to better understand an individual's behavior in response to the environment or stimuli. ABA consists of various strategies and interventions, which allow teachers and service providers many options to customize programs for each individual student (Zager, Wehmeyer, & Simpson, 2012).

ABA is based upon the A-B-C model of antecedent, behavior, and consequence. Within any ABA program, data collection and analysis are necessary components. The data collection and analysis determines whether a strategy is working or if something needs to be adjusted. Data collection in ABA must be meticulous (Webber & Scheuermann, 2008; Zager, Wehmeyer, & Simpson, 2012).

Within ABA, two of the more popular techniques include discrete trial training (DTT) and naturalistic teaching. DTT is used to teach new skills or practice previously learned skills (Zager, Wehmeyer, & Simpson, 2012). Through DTT, a skill is broken down into smaller chunks and taught step by step, ensuring that each step is mastered before moving onto the next. DTT must be well structured and utilize simple and clear instructions by the teacher or service provider (Webber & Scheuermann, 2008).

Naturalistic teaching occurs within the child's natural environment where the child's natural curiosity takes center stage. Through naturalistic teaching, the teacher proactively manipulates the environment, based upon the interests and desired activities of the student, to create teachable moments through modeling and imitation (Luiselli et al., 2008; Zager, Wehmeyer, & Simpson, 2012).

Both models, along with many other promising evidence-based practices and strategies, hold the key to helping students with ASD live more fulfilling lives. Once these students are better able to communicate and understand the world around them, they find success where once it may have eluded them.

POINTS TO REMEMBER

- *Applied behavior analysis (ABA) has been extensively researched and supported for over 50 years. Research has and continues to prove the positive effects of ABA strategies and interventions for individuals with ASD.*
- *ABA is based upon an A-B-C model, which examines antecedents, behavior, and consequences. By using the A-B-C model, teachers and service providers are able to gain a deeper understanding of a student's behaviors in relation to the student's environment.*
- *ABA relies heavily on data collection and analysis. In the beginning of any ABA treatment, data is collected and analyzed to determine functions of behaviors in order to develop an appropriate and individualized program. Once the program is implemented, data is collected frequently to track the student's progress and determine if elements of the program need to be revisited.*
- *Under the umbrella of ABA, there are many strategies and practices that are supported by extensive research including discrete trial training, naturalistic teaching, visual prompting, and scripting, to name a few.*

Chapter Seven

Developing Social Skills

Social Interactions and Social Awareness

Social reciprocity is a core deficit for those diagnosed with ASD; thus, the need for interventions that increase social skills is a key component in the development of an effective educational plan. With many types of interventions available, including those that are not research-based, it is often difficult for educators to determine the best method for helping their students develop social awareness (Radley et al., 2017). A lack of research available on specific groups with ASD, such as females and students at the secondary level, also make it challenging to know what may or may not work (Bal et al., 2015; Jamison & Schuttler, 2017; Ledford et al., 2018).

Social skills deficits can lead to a plethora of challenges for autistic students including becoming bullies or being victimized by bullies (Cappadocia, Weiss, & Pepler, 2012; Chen & Schwartz, 2012). Unstated social rules and regulations that seem easily understood by typically developing youth and adolescents are termed the *hidden curriculum* (Myles, Trautman, & Schelvan, 2013). The inability to navigate the complexities of the hidden curriculum are the most difficult for students with ASD (Myles, Trautman, & Schelvan, 2013).

SOCIAL SKILLS DEFICITS AND THE EFFECT ON STUDENTS WITH ASD

It is necessary for educators to develop an understanding of the ways in which social skills deficits affect students with ASD. Individuals with autism are often perceived as having little to no desire for social interaction, yet research suggests that the opposite is true (White, Keonig, & Scahill, 2007). Students with ASD are often eager to participate in social situations with their peers; however, due to a lack of support and intervention, standing on the periphery seems more palatable than facing the social awkwardness that is typical of their experiences (Koegel et al., 2012; White, Keonig, & Scahill, 2007).

It is not a lack of social interest, but rather an inability to determine which social conventions to use, why to use them, and when to use them that proves problematic for individuals with ASD (White, Keonig, & Scahill, 2007). Interestingly, many autistic students who are integrated into classrooms with their typically developed peers experience increased risk for peer rejection and social isolation (Jamison & Schuttler, 2017; Ostmeyer & Scarpa, 2012; White, Keonig, & Scahill, 2007). Not surprisingly, then, students who are socially ostracized tend to underperform in school and later in the workplace (White, Keonig, & Scahill, 2007).

Social skills deficits can range from the inability to initiate or maintain eye contact to more severe behaviors such as self-stimulating movements (stimming) and fixation on limited topics (Radley et al., 2017). While these behaviors may be concerning, although not overly problematic in the social world of very young children, these impairments compound over time, likely due to the complexity of age-specific social interactions (Jamison & Schuttler, 2017). In addition to becoming further ostracized from their peer groups, students with ASD can experience depression and anxiety as a result of their lack of appropriate social awareness (White, Keonig, & Scahill, 2007).

Along with developing the ability to interact with peers in an appropriate fashion, students with ASD must also increase their adaptive skills, which include the daily activities that lead to functional independence such as personal hygiene, meal preparation, time management, and obtaining employment (Bal et al., 2015). Adaptive skills and cognition are not mutually dependent. Many times, students who have high cognitive skills have low adaptive skills; yet, the need for adaptive skills training is overlooked, especially in students with high-functioning autism (Ledford et al., 2018).

It is important, therefore, to examine the individual student to determine a specific needs profile before choosing a social intervention program (Ledford et al., 2018). Factors that should be examined include the student's current level of social functioning, the severity of the social deficits, the student's ability to communicate, and the student's ability to carry out daily living skills independently (Bal et al., 2015; Ruble et al., 2010).

SOCIAL SKILLS DEFICITS AND BULLYING

Difficulties with communication and social awareness put students with autism at an increased risk for victimization from bullies (Cappadocia, Weiss, & Pepler, 2012). Bullying is a form of aggressive behavior whereby someone intentionally and repeatedly causes another person injury or discomfort; bullying can be physical or emotional and includes cyberbullying (Espelage, 2017). Students with ASD are four times more likely to be bullied than their typically developed peers (Fisher & Taylor, 2016).

Due to the nature of their disability, students with ASD have difficulty defending themselves as they often lack the social supports that may help mitigate the bullying behavior (Cappadocia, Weiss, & Pepler, 2012). Students with ASD often have fewer friendships, difficulties in communicating with others, and an inability to regulate emotions which all contribute to easy victimization by bullies (Fisher & Taylor, 2016). These factors increase the risk that autistic students will become bullies themselves or become bully–victims—students who both experience bullying and bully other students (Chen & Schwartz, 2012).

In all cases, bullying affects students' quality of life at school, often leading to depression, anxiety, and even suicidal ideation; however, for the student with ASD, the impact is often magnified by an inability to communicate the need for help (Chen & Schwartz, 2012). When it comes to reporting bullying instances, there is a disparity in the number of reports made by parents versus students themselves.

Fisher and Taylor (2016) suggest the disparity could exist for many reasons including embarrassment in reporting victimization as well as a misunderstanding of ill-intentioned behavior, leaving the student unsure as to whether he or she is being bullied. Students who are bullied often keep their victimization to themselves, which leads to internalizing symptoms, which can manifest as self-injurious behavior (Adams et al., 2014; Zablotsky et al., 2014).

Bullying does not only occur toward students in separate settings. Even when students with ASD are placed in inclusive settings, the instances of becoming targets for bullies often intensify (Zablotsky et al., 2014). Proper supports are crucial to ensure that the likelihood of victimization of an autistic student remains low (Ruble et al., 2010).

Bullying can often spread quickly throughout a school if educators and administrators fail to take the proper steps necessary to put an end to bullying (Afach, Kiwan, & Semaan, 2018). In the case of cyberbullying in particular, students with ASD can be the easiest targets because of the ambiguity of roles in the virtual world and often the difficulty in tracking down the perpetrators.

SOCIAL SKILLS DEFICITS AND LIFE SKILLS

While younger children with ASD may benefit from early intervention in adaptive living skills, such as brushing their teeth, proper toileting, and dressing themselves appropriately, these skills become more of an issue during puberty. Autistic adolescents often start experiencing increased social awareness difficulties around the same time that they begin to experience physiological and hormonal changes (Plexousakis, Georgiadi, & Kourkoutas, 2011). As hormonal changes occur, typically developed adolescents begin to explore sexuality and relationships; however, for a child with ASD, these changes often present confusion as the child is unsure how to express his or her new feelings (Plexousakis, Georgiadi, & Kourkoutas, 2011). Particularly in girls with ASD, the increasing impact of self-care on developing adolescent relationships can be difficult to manage (Jamison & Schuttler, 2017).

As adolescents are developing a sense of themselves and exploring their identities, the change in physiology often comes at a price to the development of new relationships. For instance, in many cases, adolescents with ASD have difficulty understanding why self-care measures are important. This can further ostracize them from their peers (Jamison & Schuttler, 2017). Individuals with autism may also have sensory issues that make it difficult to participate in activities such as bathing or handwashing because of the negative sensory input they receive from such activities (National Autistic Society, 2017).

As with other forms of social skills training, daily living skills can be developed through the use of traditional forms of intervention. Something as basic as a visual checklist can help children with ASD remember to perform personal care activities (Autism Speaks, 2012). This can be especially helpful in school settings where students may not generalize the activities they do at home into the educational environment, such as washing hands after using the bathroom.

A critical component to the successful development of daily living skills is consistency (Plexousakis, Georgiadi, & Kourkoutas, 2011). Keeping a consistent routine at home and school—and ensuring that communication between home and school occurs on a regular basis—is critical in helping autistic children become more independent with their self-care.

WHEN SOCIAL SKILLS INTERVENTIONS DO NOT WORK

For many reasons, social skills interventions that are designed to increase prosocial interactions for students with ASD often fall short (Ledford et al., 2018; Murphy, Radley, & Helbig, 2018; Radley et al., 2017). Evidence-based practices in social intervention are likely to result in positive outcomes for students with ASD; however, when it comes to collecting data to gauge the practice's effectiveness, educators have often failed to implement the program correctly, resulting in invalid results (Ledford et al., 2018). This is not predominantly the fault of the educator. Evidence-based practices may not be utilized as often as they should be because of a lack of training for the practitioner, limited time to employ the practice, a lack of resources to spend on social curriculum, and/or a lack of professional development opportunities for practitioners (Radley et al., 2017).

The three biggest obstacles to effective social skills training have little to do with practitioner knowledge. Research suggests that a lack of generalization from program to real-life application, a lack of individualized, targeted instruction, and a lack of relevance to specific subgroups of the autistic population affects the efficacy of increased social development for students on the autism spectrum (Bal et al., 2015; Cridland et al., 2014; Ledford et al., 2018; Radley et al., 2017).

The shortcomings in social skills programs hinder practitioners from gaining the data needed to make explicit and informed educational plans for their students. In many cases, one-size-fits-all approaches have the exact opposite effect on social skill development, causing students to regress in their development (Dingfelder & Mandell, 2011). This is especially true when looking at programs that do not generalize skills, lack a targeted approach to prosocial skills, and do not address the groups of students who most need assistance.

Lack of Generalization

Programs that purport to help autistic students gain social awareness often lack the components to provide generalization of skills across domains (Murphy, Radley, & Helbig, 2018). In most instances, typical social skills training focuses on teaching incremental social skills through a step-by-step role-play method. These role-playing methods often occur in a pullout setting between the student and instructor, or in a small group of students with similar social deficits (Radley et al., 2017). While the student may show improvements in skills within that particular environment, he or she often cannot make the generalization to other environments, especially in situations that are novel to the student (Murphy, Radley, & Helbig, 2018; Radley et al., 2017).

When students leave the safety of the social skills group, they are often overwhelmed by the need to not only interact in unexpected settings, but to remember the strategies they learned in the group. While many groups include typically developed peers to promote a more naturalistic approach to social interactions, there are a large number of groups that include only students who share similar deficits (Radley et al., 2017). Without the exposure to unfamiliar situations with typically developed peers, students with ASD may make little progress toward increased skills development.

Lack of Specific Targeted Interventions

Another challenge standing in the way of increasing social skills development in students with ASD is a lack of specific, targeted intervention toward explicit prosocial behaviors. Using broad approaches with the aim of increasing social awareness has little effect on students' overall progress (Ledford et al., 2018). Dingfelder and Mandell (2011) argue that without a social skills curriculum that targets specific behaviors, any intervention may actually impede the progress of increased skills that will lead to better social awareness.

Interventions that are both evidence-based and easy to use for the practitioner should be incorporated into all social skills training initiatives (Radley et al., 2017). In fact, researchers and technicians have been moving toward developing software that can work better than traditional social skills programs to increase social learning in students with ASD (Esposito et al., 2017). These types of interventions take evidence-based practices and incorporate them into an easier-to-use format for children and adolescents.

Lack of Relevance to Specific Groups

In addition to targeting explicit social learning such as pragmatics, prosody, and personal space awareness, as well as daily living skills such as personal care and time management, prosocial interventions must also teach students about such personal issues as relationships, sexuality, and puberty (Jamison & Schuttler, 2017). Many interventions fall short in this area because they mainly focus on the elementary school population (Jamison & Schuttler, 2017).

Students who are in the high-functioning category of autism often appear to understand these topics in a similar manner to their typically developed peers (Cridland et al., 2014). In turn, this leads to these students being overlooked and being left to navigate society without added supports. The two most affected groups are females and students in secondary school.

Females with ASD

While the research surrounding boys with ASD is substantial, girls with ASD are often overlooked (Cridland et al., 2014). There are many reasons for this deficit in the research. Some studies suggest girls with ASD often have lower IQs and, as a result, are diagnosed with disabilities that are intellectual in nature (Cridland et al., 2014; Nichols, Moravcik, & Tetenbaum, 2009). The associated symptomology with autism is then overlooked because the cognitive factor appears to have the bigger impact on the student's functioning.

Girls tend to have stronger social skills than their male counterparts; that is, girls often have a seemingly easier time engaging in pretend play scenarios, social initiation, and communication (Baron-Cohen et al., 2011; Cridland et al., 2014; Nichols, Moravcik, & Tetenbaum, 2009). As social complexities grow with age, girls with ASD often find themselves unable to relate to the same peers they may have connected with in elementary school. Adolescence brings on role changes for peers and at this stage there is a shift in dependence from the parent to the peer group (Jamison & Schuttler, 2017).

For females with ASD, this change can lead to poor self-esteem, depression, and increased victimization from bullies because they often do not understand the hidden social cues that are understood by their typically developed peers (Cridland et al., 2014; Jamison & Schuttler, 2017). Since girls often experience puberty before boys, the added stressors of self-care, biological changes, and concerns about appearance can increase females' need for supports in all domains of social awareness (Jamison & Schuttler, 2017).

Students in Secondary School

As students get older and move from elementary to middle school, there is an absence of programs that address the skills needed for this population. Research suggests curriculums that are based on the acquisition of basic skills such as turn taking, expressing wants and needs, and basic conversational skills can benefit older students (Bal et al., 2015; Jamison & Schuttler, 2017; Murphy, Radley, & Helbig, 2018).

To successfully monitor student progress, however, practitioners must take care to teach these skills in a way that is generalizable to more age-appropriate situations, such as appreciating differing perspectives, discussing the interests of others, and increasing independent decision making (Jamison & Schuttler, 2017; Murphy, Radley, & Helbig, 2018). These types of strategies can become powerful interventions for older students with ASD (Hughes et al., 2012). Social problem solving and self-management instruction can help older students to work through the common challenges they may face in a typical adolescent social situation (Hughes et al., 2012).

For instance, high school students who were provided with direct instruction in conversational skills were able to generalize this skill in a more spontaneous construct (Davis et al., 2010). These high school students were taught using a method that is traditionally used with younger children—reinforcement through superheroes—but was modified for the needs of the high school student (Davis et al., 2010). The students were able to apply the learned strategies to increase their ability to maintain an appropriate two-sided conversation with peers (Hughes et al., 2012).

With regard to self-management, students with ASD who have strong peer models are better able to understand the difference between socially appropriate and inappropriate behavior (Hughes et al., 2012; Radley et al., 2017; White, Keonig, & Scahill, 2007). In a study examining the Girls Night Out (GNO) program, for example, adolescent girls who participated in intervention measures designed to promote natural socialization with groups of peers within their community demonstrated increased social awareness and self-perception (Jamison & Schuttler, 2017). That is not to say that similar interventions will show success in all instances of social skills training; however, the results are promising (Hughes et al., 2012; Jamison & Schuttler, 2017; Murphy, Radley, & Helbig, 2018).

CONSIDERATIONS FOR IMPROVING SOCIAL AWARENESS

As with any new skill, practice makes perfect. Providing opportunities for children and adolescents with ASD to practice new social skills in natural settings with same-aged peers is crucial for their successful transition into independence in adulthood (Bal et al., 2015; Murphy, Radley, & Helbig, 2018; Radley et al., 2017). It is often challenging to determine the best method of intervention for any given student, as what is successful for one may not be helpful for all.

Myriad social skills interventions that have shown effectiveness for students with ASD are included for review. It is important to note that this list is not complete; rather the list includes a selection of interventions that are research-based and hold promise on the large scale (Esposito et al.; 2017; Jamison & Schuttler, 2017; Larsen & Samdal, 2012; Radley et al., 2017; Withey, 2017).

The Superheroes Social Skills Program

Designed to provide school-based social skills training for students with ASD, this program requires little specialized training and can be implemented by a wide range of school staff (Radley et al., 2017). The program uses many evidence-based strategies, such as video modeling, self-monitoring, and social stories to teach students the ways in which to use skills in a safe setting and how to generalize them into novel settings (Murphy, Radley, & Helbig, 2018).

Toca Boca

Toca Boca, a Swedish game development studio, aims to engage children in the types of social themes they are likely to experience as they mature (Toca Boca, 2018). There are 40 different types of interactive Toca Boca games that deal with everything from grocery shopping to pet care. The games purport to allow children "the freedom to play in ways that only they can dream up" (Toca Boca, 2018). The interactivity of the game modules encourage players to experiment with different roles (e.g., office worker, hospital patient, hair stylist, etc.). The various games may align with social–emotional IEP goals by teaching such concepts as sharing and turn-taking (Withey, 2017).

TeachTown

TeachTown is another interactive platform that allows children with ASD and other developmental and intellectual disabilities to improve academic, behavioral, and adaptive functioning; the software is appropriate for children in elementary school all the way through postsecondary education (Teach-Town, 2018). The program uses evidence-based ABA approaches—such as prompting, fading, or increasing distractors—and positive reinforcement, to deliver high-quality instruction via an interactive and engaging computer program (Esposito et al., 2017; TeachTown, 2018). The program also purports to assist with generalization of skills through a system of increasing difficulty as a child masters a skill (Esposito et al., 2017).

Girls Night Out (GNO)

GNO is a social skills training program with the goal of improving self-confidence and self-perception in girls with ASD (Jamison & Schuttler, 2017). The success of the program is based on the interaction between girls with ASD and their typically developed peers. The creators' aim is for girls to develop functional social and adaptive skills that will lead to increased self-esteem and better social–emotional health (Jamison & Schuttler, 2017). Families of participants of the program state that it helped to increase their child's confidence levels by allowing interaction with same-aged girls in typical social settings. The GNO sessions occur in the general community to allow for participants to practice their skills in a variety of settings (Jamison & Schuttler, 2017).

Second Step

Second Step is a social skills training program developed by the Committee for Children (2018) that targets early childhood through middle school ages. The program incorporates skill training in the areas of social–emotional learning, bullying prevention, and abuse awareness (Committee for Children, 2018). Although the Second Step program is appropriate for children of all ability levels, the advantage to the program is that it can be regularly embedded into an existing curriculum. The developers provide weekly lessons with daily activities that help to teach and reinforce necessary social skills for all students (Committee for Children, 2018). The program uses a mix of textbooks, computer software, and videos to help educators approach sensitive subjects (e.g., abuse and trauma) while providing strategies to help students understand and cope.

FINAL THOUGHTS

Social skills deficits can affect students with ASD in myriad ways to include bullying, social ostracizing, decreased self-worth, depression, and anxiety (Jamison & Schuttler, 2017; White, Keonig, & Scahill, 2007). The need for effective interventions is crucial as a means to help individuals with ASD become better able to navigate the social complexities of the world around them. Beginning with the development of the IEP, educators must critically examine the areas of need for their students and build a specialized program targeting skills deficits, specifically those that require reading others' emotions and intentions (Myles, Trautman, & Schelvan, 2013).

It is also necessary for educators and others who work with children and adolescents with ASD to realize that these individuals are not choosing to remain on the periphery of their peer groups (White, Keonig, & Scahill, 2007). Instead, children—and especially adolescents with ASD—very much want to be included in social situations with their peers, yet the fear of rejection and failure is often too overwhelming (Koegel et al., 2012). The same skills deficits are not shared in all individuals with ASD, making it all the more challenging to determine the best approach for improving social skills.

For a variety of reasons, many social skills interventions fall short when it comes to increasing prosocial behaviors in students with ASD; however, there are some promising interventions that have been shown to promote social awareness growth for individuals with ASD (Ledford et al., 2018; Murphy, Radley, & Helbig, 2018; Radley et al., 2017). The hope is that educators will become familiar with some of the most effective interventions and use them with fidelity to help improve outcomes for students with ASD. While none of these interventions is a panacea to the social and communication deficits characteristic of autism, many of these programs show promise in helping individuals with autism access social norms in ways similar to their typically developing peers.

POINTS TO REMEMBER

- *Social skills deficits can lead to several challenges for students with ASD including feelings of victimization from bullying, depression, low self-esteem, and even suicidal ideations (Cappadocia, Weiss, & Pepler, 2012; Jamison & Schuttler, 2017; Ostmeyer & Scarpa, 2012).*

- *In addition to a decreased ability to appropriately interact socially with peers, students with ASD can suffer from deficits in adaptive skills such as personal hygiene, time management, and meal preparation (Bal et al., 2015).*
- *Individuals with high-functioning autism are often viewed as "normal-looking" and so they tend to be overlooked as candidates for intervention programs (Ledford et al., 2018).*
- *There are many reasons why social skills interventions are not always successful; however, a lack of generalization, a lack of individualized instruction, and a lack of relevance for specific groups of autistic individuals are the three biggest challenges to effective social skills training (Bal et al., 2015; Cridland et al., 2014; Ledford et al., 2018; Radley et al., 2017).*
- *When considering interventions for students with ASD, educators must account for the opportunities for the student to practice his or her newly developing skills as well as the ability to utilize these skills in a naturalistic setting (Bal et al., 2015; Murphy, Radley, & Helbig, 2018; Radley et al., 2017; White, Keonig, & Scahill, 2007).*

Chapter Eight

Effective Collaboration with Related Service Providers

The Importance of Teamwork

Students with ASD are a unique group of individuals in that they often require assistance from a wide range of professionals who provide services in areas such as speech development, fine and gross motor skills, behavior analysis, and mental health assistance in order to make progress in both academic and functional life skills. Children with ASD, however, are much more likely than children with any other category of disability to have difficulty accessing care, therefore resulting in poor outcomes for early developmental intervention (Brookman-Frazee, Drahota, & Stadnick, 2012). This gap in access places a crushing financial and emotional burden on the families of these children, as they are tasked with paying out-of-pocket costs for intervention and special health care needs (Brookman-Frazee, Drahota, & Stadnick, 2012).

The earlier the identification of ASD, the better the chance of successful intervention (Cameron & Muskett, 2014). When children are identified in the early stages of development, families have timely access to service providers and intervention programs that may improve outcomes for their children; yet many children are not diagnosed at an early age, making it difficult for families to obtain appropriate services (Cameron & Muskett, 2014; Reichow, 2012). Furthermore, research suggests that there is a shortage of quality community mental health and other service providers that are qualified to work with this unique population, making it even more difficult for families to find help once their child receives a diagnosis of ASD (Brookman-Frazee, Drahota, & Stadnick, 2012; Cameron & Muskett, 2014).

School-based related service providers play a pivotal role in providing students with ASD access to key services to increase skill development (Hart Barnett & O'shaughnessy, 2015; Kelly & Tincani, 2013). The most common service providers seen in schools include speech-language therapists, occupational therapists, physical therapists, and school-based counseling services, which often provide social skills training and other assistance with fundamental life skills. Yet many of these service providers have difficulty ensuring that services are being delivered in a consistent manner and with fidelity (Hart Barnett & O'shaughnessy, 2015).

Often service professionals and educators lack the ability to collaborate effectively, either through a lack of training or a lack of time to create meaningful plans of action. Researchers suggest there are ways to mitigate the challenges of effective collaboration through increased communication and appreciation of the roles each educator and service provider plays in the development of the autistic student (Brookman-Frazee, Drahota, & Stadnick, 2012; Hart Barnett & O'shaughnessy, 2015; Kelly & Tincani, 2013).

UNDERSTANDING THE ROLE OF THE SERVICE PROVIDER

Occupational Therapists

Occupational therapists (OTs) provide services in fine motor development, sensory processing, and social skills development. Students on the autism spectrum often exhibit challenges participating appropriately in play opportunities, communicating effectively, and developing functional life skills; OTs have the ability to touch upon all of these skills deficits in their work (Hart Barnett & O'shaughnessy, 2015).

According to the American Occupational Therapy Association (AOTA) (2018), children's lives are made up of "occupations" such as playing, learning, and socializing. OTs are able to help children make significant gains in these areas by helping them to develop routines, deal with sensory needs, and increase fine motor skills for school-based and functional living tasks, such as cutting or buttoning clothing (American Occupational Therapy Association, 2018).

For young children with autism, the OT's main role is to provide evaluation of developmentally appropriate skills and determine whether further services would help to enhance the child's sensorimotor performance, sensory processing, and social–behavioral performance (Hart Barnett & O'shaughnessy, 2015). These skills can be worked on in school-based settings and then carried over into the home and community. As children age, they begin to develop more intense needs that OTs can address. As social demands become more complex for adolescents and young adults on the spectrum, OTs can help these individuals develop effective planning strategies for time management, managing uncomfortable sensory experiences, and navigating novel social interactions (American Occupational Therapy Association, 2018).

OTs can help with sensory processing difficulties as well. As many children with ASD have challenges with movement, touch, smell, and sound, OTs can identify these areas of difficulty and develop plans where the slow integration of sensory stimuli help the child's brain to reprocess the incoming sensory information in a way that is less jarring to the student (Autism Speaks, 2018h). This type of therapy helps students become less distracted by sensory overload and readier to participate in learning tasks. Sensory processing strategies as taught by an OT can also help to calm a child who is experiencing behavioral outbursts (Autism Speaks, 2018h). Sensory processing disorders have been linked to anxiety in children with ASD; therefore, it is important to teach strategies that can alleviate negative feelings of stress when confronted with novel situations (Case-Smith, Weaver, & Fristad, 2015).

Speech-Language Therapists

Speech-language therapists (SLTs) play an important role in assisting students with ASD in the development of increased receptive and expressive language skills (Smith & Gillon, 2004). As deficits in social communication are a key characteristic of an autism diagnosis, SLTs are sought after to provide early intervention services as well as continued therapeutic supports to students on all portions of the autism spectrum (Cameron & Muskett, 2014). Speech-language therapy is designed to address not only the mechanics of speech, but also the social pragmatics of language (Autism Speaks, 2018g).

All children with ASD have vastly different profiles; thus, examining each student on a case-by-case basis is necessary for determining the level of need for speech-language services. For instance, in many students with ASD, nonverbal and nonsocial problem-solving skills tend to emerge as relative strengths (Smith & Gillon, 2004). These children are able to complete tasks that require higher levels of visual–spatial integration, such as solving puzzles.

Tasks that require the ability to understand abstract concepts, however, especially in ways that necessitate the application of language in nuanced forms, prove particularly challenging for students with ASD (Autism Speaks, 2018g; Smith & Gillon, 2004). For students with this profile, SLTs will often utilize traditional social skills strategies to assist the students with the acquisition and appropriate use of language (Smith & Gillon, 2004). SLTs will often work with students in small groups to promote increased social awareness, but they may also work individually with students who are experiencing severe deficits in language acquisition (Autism Speaks, 2018g).

Additionally, SLTs are often the point people for working with augmentative and alternative communication devices (AACs). In particular, autistic students who are nonverbal have shown benefits from using AACs to develop functional communication skills (Boyd, Hart Barnett, & More, 2015; Shane et al., 2012; Xin & Leonard, 2014). SLTs are pivotal in instructing educators in the best ways to incorporate AACs into the classroom. One of the most widely used AACs in use today is the Picture Exchange Communication System (PECS). Instructors and therapists help the nonverbal student learn how to exchange a picture for an object in order to begin to form sentences (Smith & Gillon, 2004). The program is helpful for nonverbal students who cannot convey their wants and needs with traditional speech, as it helps them to develop a system of communication in place of what often becomes physical aggression.

Behavior Analysts

In recent years, applied behavior analysis (ABA) has become the preferred method of working with students with ASD. ABA has shown effectiveness for students with ASD in several ways including teaching new skills, increasing appropriate social and adaptive behaviors, generalizing and transferring behaviors across contexts, and reducing behavioral responses to novelty (e.g., self-injurious behavior, stereotyped movements, etc.) (Kelly & Tincani, 2013; Smith, 2012).

As a discipline, ABA is rapidly growing. In 2007, the Behavior Analyst Certification Board reported an approximate 90% increase in the number of Board Certified Behavior Analysts (BCBAs) and Board Certified Assistant Behavior Analysts (BCaBAs) between the years 2000 and 2007 (Kelly & Tincani, 2013). Many states require behavior analysts who work with students who are autistic to become licensed by the governing board of their profession (Kelly & Tincani, 2013).

BCBAs and BCaBAs are crucial members of an autistic student's multidisciplinary team. These professionals' role is to evaluate programming and develop behavior plans for students in all educational settings. They are tasked with helping educators and other service providers with understanding the ways in which to utilize behavior modification strategies in order to help students with ASD develop more appropriate responses to stressors in their environment (Kelly & Tincani, 2013). It is essential that behavior analysts work collaboratively with educational staff to discover the root causes of an individual child's behavior (Smith, 2012).

Community Mental Health (CMH) Therapists

Not all services needed by autistic students can be received in the school setting. There are several outside agencies that work collaboratively with schools to provide a continuum of therapy. CMH therapists continue to play an important role in assisting autistic children and their families to find and receive appropriate behavioral and mental health treatment (Brookman-Frazee, Drahota, & Stadnick, 2012).

Many children with ASD also have comorbid disorders that need treatment, ranging from anxiety disorders to schizophrenia (Bryson et al., 2008; Mattila et al., 2010). This type of treatment cannot easily be provided by school-based therapists who lack clinical training (Brookman-Frazee, Drahota, & Stadnick, 2012). CMH therapists can assist in developing treatment plans that can be shared with the school to help with the incorporation of strategies that will allow for the easier management of symptoms from co-occurring disorders.

CMH therapists working with the autistic population also face substantial challenges in providing effective treatment to these individuals. In many cases, CMH therapists themselves lack training in working with the autistic population. Coupled with the brevity with which many of these practitioners see patients, it becomes difficult to see improvements in patient outcomes (Brookman-Frazee, Taylor, & Garland, 2010; Brookman-Frazee, Drahota, & Stadnick, 2012).

It often takes a substantial amount of time to receive CMH services due to an already overloaded system, and so, children who desperately need therapeutic intervention face long wait times to receive assistance (Brookman-Frazee, Drahota, & Stadnick, 2012). Once those services are approved and rendered, it is not unusual for results to take longer to be visible, which can further frustrate both families and educators. It is for this reason that it is critical for CMH services to collaborate with schools to ensure that a continuum of services is in place for the students receiving assistance from these agencies.

COLLABORATION STRATEGIES FOR SERVICE PROVIDERS AND EDUCATORS

In order to ensure maximum benefit to students of any age with ASD, collaboration between service providers and educators must occur (Hart Barnett & O'shaughnessy, 2015; Friend & Cook, 2013). There are several challenges to successful collaboration including service providers' heavy caseloads, time constraints that affect planning time, and the inability for educators to devote time for occupational therapy strategies due to fast-paced curriculum and testing demands (Hart Barnett & O'shaughnessy, 2015).

With respect to students with ASD in general education inclusion classrooms, collaboration between the educator and the service provider is necessary to ensure a truly inclusive experience for all students (Boshoff & Stewart, 2013; Friend & Cook, 2013). It is also important for educators to recognize that many of the practices used by service providers are based on universal design which can benefit students of all ability levels, leading to increased outcomes for all students (American Occupational Therapy Association, 2018).

Developing effective communication skills is the first step in ensuring that successful collaboration is taking place. Educators and service providers must actively listen to each other's perspectives and appreciate the levels of experience and knowledge each practitioner brings to the table. Educators work with their students for approximately 30-plus hours per week, and related service providers may only see the same students for one to two hours per week; it is important to understand that each professional has unique knowledge that is critical to developing a well-rounded plan of intervention (Hart Barnett & O'shaughnessy, 2015).

Respect for each professional's perspective is the best way to facilitate the most effective plan of action for students with ASD. Given that most educators and service providers are under enormous pressure to serve large numbers of students, it is often challenging to find the time to communicate. Developing a communication system that includes multiple contact methods, especially those that utilize technology (e.g., text messaging, Skyping, email), can be instrumental in maintaining open dialogue about the needs of students (Boshoff & Stewart, 2013).

Another key piece to effective collaboration involves time to co-plan. Many educators and service providers have limited time for co-planning, and so they often play it by ear when it comes to implementing strategies within the classroom. Co-planning requires deliberate and structured meeting times that are devoted to examining a student's profile, evaluating the student's progress on existing interventions, and developing improved plans of action for delivering more effective instruction (Friend & Cook, 2013).

More often than not, educators and service providers engage in off-the-cuff conversations that are fit in during transition periods. This is often the only time that these professionals can collaborate and it becomes problematic, as effective planning cannot take place when neither person is ready for the conversation (Hart Barnett & O'shaughnessy, 2015). Friend and Cook (2013) suggest that at least one hour per week of co-planning is recommended for successful collaboration between educators and service providers.

In order to make the best use of co-planning time, educators and service providers should create and stick to an agenda with key points and concerns (Friend & Cook, 2013). Following an outline of concerns will help with shared decision making, for example, the most appropriate times to observe students, or the best ways in which to incorporate behavior strategies into existing lessons (Kelly & Tincani, 2013).

Scheduled observation periods also allow for service providers to obtain useful information in a systematic way about the students with whom they work. Scheduling times for service providers to observe students within the classroom allows providers to understand if their recommendations are working as well as to determine whether their recommendations are being followed in the classroom. This gives the provider a chance to reassess the student informally and make changes to strategies as necessary (Hart Barnett & O'shaughnessy, 2015).

Although service providers may only work with one or two students in a given classroom, it is important to recognize that the strategies the service provider uses to teach life skills to those students can be applied to students regardless of disability. Universal design for learning (UDL) principles suggest that the design of instructional materials, activities, and assessments can be created in such a way as to benefit all learners (Gargiulo, 2015; CAST, 2018).

UDL gives equal opportunity and access to all learners. Instead of providing a one-size-fits-all type of approach, UDL can be customized to the learner's needs (CAST, 2018). Key pieces of UDL include presenting information and content in different ways that make sense for different types of learners, allowing students to express their knowledge in learning in differentiated ways, and finding ways in which to motivate and engage students based on their interest and prior knowledge (National Center on Universal Design for Learning, 2014).

Teachers are generally given the freedom to differentiate their instruction in the classroom to accommodate the various learning styles of their students. Service providers are also given that latitude, especially when working with students in the inclusion setting. Yet, one of the obstacles to effective collaboration occurs when service providers who work with students in the inclusion setting often find themselves and the student working in isolation. This can be detrimental for student growth as students are afforded few opportunities to practice their skills with their peers. Additionally, working in isolation singles out the student as being different from his or her peers.

Ideally, employing UDL principles is an effective way of reducing the need for increased services outside the classroom. Behavior analysts, SLTs, and OTs can offer useful consultative services in lieu of direct services for educators who are willing and able to carry out strategies within the classroom (Hart Barnett & O'shaughnessy, 2015; Kelly & Tincani, 2013). UDL techniques can also reduce the amount of time a student is segregated from his or her peers in order to receive direct service.

UDL principles can be applied to all areas of the curriculum; thus, the chances of singling out one student based on his or her need for service decreases. If all students are using a computer for a written assignment, for example, a student with ASD might utilize the accessibility features that provide access to accommodations such as auditory feedback, keyboarding assistance, and larger font (Hart Barnett & O'shaughnessy, 2015).

This practice also alleviates the stress that the teacher often feels when only one student needs related services. In utilizing UDL, the teacher can plan for the whole class's needs, including the student requiring related services, without planning for a separate method of instruction (Hart Barnett & O'shaughnessy, 2015; CAST, 2018).

Collaboration should be encouraged between related service providers as well. Many service providers work in isolation, rarely getting the opportunity to collaborate with providers from other areas of specialty. With the exception of the multidisciplinary team meeting, most service providers only see each other in passing, never really sitting down to talk about the ways in which their services interrelate, or how they can possibly team up for the better provision of services.

This is especially true for school-based providers and CMH providers who often have limited knowledge of their clients. Treatment plans could be better developed with increased collaboration between CMH providers and school staff (Brookman-Frazee, Drahota, & Stadnick, 2012). Similarly, collaboration between school and community providers can help with the implementation and sustainability of effective treatment options for students with ASD, especially those with comorbid conditions that require more intense psychiatric care (Brookman-Frazee, Drahota, & Stadnick, 2012; Mattila et al., 2010).

Many schools have adopted the practice of allowing community providers to see their clients at the school. This makes it easier for students in need to receive a continuum of services without the added stress of finding additional time and transportation; however, community providers should be regarded as essential members of the student's team and should be incorporated to the largest extent possible into collaborative meetings and planning times.

FINAL THOUGHTS

Students with ASD are likely to require additional support services from related service providers such as speech-language therapists, occupational therapists, and behavior analysts. Given the nature of their disability, students with ASD often need intensive social and communication support that cannot easily be provided by the special education teacher alone. Further related services may be needed from community health providers who work with both the student and family (Brookman-Frazee, Drahota, & Stadnick, 2012).

Early identification of a need for services allows for better chances at access to a well-rounded continuum of services that will ultimately help to improve the student's outcomes (Cameron & Muskett, 2014; Reichow, 2012). A shortage of community providers who are qualified to work with autistic students, coupled with school-based related service providers who have crushing caseloads, mean that many students with ASD are unable to access the services they need (Brookman-Frazee, Drahota, & Stadnick, 2012; Cameron & Muskett, 2014). Collaboration between service providers and educators is key to ensuring that students with ASD have access to the most effective services possible.

Successful collaboration requires planning and time. While there will likely never be enough time for providers and educators to devote themselves to the types of analysis necessary to ensure rapid progress for each student receiving services, it is essential that providers and educators carve out time to truly examine the needs of each student and plan for the best ways to incorporate services and strategies into the student's everyday curriculum in order to promote progress (Hart Barnett & O'shaughnessy, 2015).

Beginning with strategies that can be applied to all students, service providers can increase the amount of time spent on each child indirectly as well as increase the quality of service through the teacher's fidelity of practice. For students who require more intense services, collaboration among all members of the multidisciplinary team is critical for developing the most effective treatment plan. Team collaboration is key in creating increased learning outcomes for students with ASD. Working together is in the best interest of the student, and this will lead to more successful futures for students with ASD.

POINTS TO REMEMBER

- *The earlier the identification of ASD, the better the chance of successful interventions (Cameron & Muskett, 2014).*
- *When a diagnosis of autism is delayed, it makes it much more difficult for families to obtain community intervention services (Brookman-Frazee, Drahota, & Stadnick, 2012).*
- *School-based related service providers play a pivotal role in helping students with ASD access the curriculum.*
- *In order to ensure that related services are being provided throughout the child's curriculum and with fidelity, collaboration between service providers and educators is key (Hart Barnett & O'shaughnessy, 2015).*

- *Communication, co-planning, observation, and utilizing UDL practices can help team members continue services indirectly in the absence of the service providers (Gargiulo, 2015; CAST, 2018; Kelly & Tincani, 2013).*

Chapter Nine

Working with Families of Autistic Students

Understanding and Coping with the Stressors

Families of students on the autism spectrum have a variety of stressors that affect them daily. Beginning with the diagnosis, family members are tasked with difficult emotional responses (Searing, Graham, & Grainger, 2015; Tint & Weiss, 2016). It is natural and expected that family members, especially mothers, will go through the grieving process once learning their child has autism; however, once the family accepts the diagnosis, there are myriad stressors family members must face in order to effectively support their autistic child (Boushey, 2001).

Although an autism diagnosis does not affect all family members equally, research suggests that everyone in the family—siblings, parents, grandparents, and extended family members—are affected in some way (Miranda et al., 2015; Searing, Graham, & Grainger, 2015; Tint & Weiss, 2016). Due to the nature of an ASD diagnosis, the needs of the child often take the forefront of the family's priorities, resulting in reduced attention to their own well-being (Tint & Weiss, 2016).

Family caregivers must often reduce the number of hours they work, pay out-of-pocket costs for health care and other services, and limit the number of commitments to others. This can be especially straining on family members, causing difficulties within same-family relationships (Tint & Weiss, 2016; Walton, 2016). Siblings of autistic children may begin to act out both at home and in school, causing added stress on the family (Walton, 2016). There is also research to suggest that marriages in families with autistic children may be strained, potentially resulting in higher divorce rates than among marriages of typically developed children (Ramisch, 2012).

DEALING WITH GRIEF

Similar to dealing with death and divorce—arguably the two most stressful events for individuals—finding out one's child has a disability is devastating news. For parents of children with ASD, the news is especially unsettling because autism has many levels and characteristics that can change over the course of each phase of a child's development (Russa, Matthews, & Owen-DeSchryver, 2015). When parents are given the news that their child has autism, they often experience the cycle of grief. Although everyone experiences grief differently, there are specific levels that are indicative of moving through the process.

In 1969, Elisabeth Kübler-Ross, a Swiss–American psychiatrist, introduced the world to the five stages of grief: denial, anger, bargaining, depression, and acceptance (Allred, 2015; Haley et al., 2013). Although this method of labeling the stages of grief has been disputed, there are certainly similarities between Kübler-Ross's model and the experiences of families who receive a disability diagnosis (Allred, 2015).

Denial/Shock

While each family who receives a diagnosis of ASD for their child will go through these stages uniquely, the majority of families begin with the shock/denial phase. Receiving the news of an autism diagnosis can be extremely overwhelming for a family to consider. In many cases, families are blindsided by the news simply because they have not seen any indicators that would lead them to believe their child is on the spectrum (Boushey, 2001). Often, this has more to do with families' lack of knowledge regarding autism and less about the symptomatology expressed by the child. Conversely, families may have an idea that something is different about their child, and while hearing the diagnosis of autism is a relief in some cases, the realities of the future become extremely overwhelming for families (Boushey, 2001; Miranda et al., 2015).

Along with shock comes denial. No family wants to accept that their child has a disability, especially one that affects him or her in every aspect of development (Boushey, 2001). Often family members will dispute testing results or withhold special education services for their child because they feel there must be another, less-devastating reason for their child's struggles (Boushey, 2001).

This creates even more challenges for the student and family as research suggests access to early intervention is needed in order to increase positive outcomes for students with ASD (Cameron & Muskett, 2014; Reichow, 2012). Service providers and school staff must be careful that they do not inadvertently alienate the families of newly diagnosed children by being overly persistent that they accept the diagnosis and move forward.

Anger

Hearing that one's child is different and will face challenges for the rest of his or her life is anger-inducing. Parents report directing their anger toward the world, toward God, and toward other family members (Boushey, 2001). Parents are also angry at themselves, often feeling as though there is something that they could have done to prevent their child's disability (Conrad, 2015; Boushey, 2001).

Anger is necessary in that it is a stabilizing emotion that allows parents to connect the diagnosis to something or someone tangible (Kessler, 2018). Anger gives parents an outlet to manage their grief with which they are familiar. In times of anger, it is essential that parents have strong support systems—whether they be formal or informal—to help navigate their feelings and turn emotions into positive action (Searing, Graham, & Grainger, 2015).

Bargaining

Bargaining with oneself or with God is a regularly occurring phase of the grief process. Many parents feel that if they change something about themselves or their current routine, such as health, environment, or education, then their child will get better (Boushey, 2001). During this phase parents often ask themselves "what if" questions that can lead to self-blame (Kessler, 2018). The truth, however, is that there is no current research to support a definitive diagnosis of autism, other than to suggest that it stems from multiple factors that may combine to increase the risk of developing neurodevelopmental impairments (Kessler, 2018).

No matter what a parent may or may not have done, it would likely not have changed their child's diagnosis; even if there was something that could have prevented the diagnosis, it does not change the current diagnosis. Parents need support to help them focus their energies on understanding *how* to help their child navigate the world instead of trying to understand *why* the child has the condition (Boushey, 2001).

Depression

Facing a lifelong disability is a depressing prospect. Parents and caregivers of children with ASD experience severe emotional and financial burdens compared to the families of typically developed children (Russa et al., 2015;

Tint & Weiss, 2016). Depression in the face of a disability diagnosis manifests itself similarly to the depression felt over losing a loved one. A sense of emptiness invades the lives of parents, and they often have difficulty moving forward (Kessler, 2018).

In a sense, having a child diagnosed with a lifelong disability is a loss. Parents' hope is that their child will not have to struggle in life, and the thought of a life filled with social and communication deficits and limited independence almost feels like a loss for both the parent and the child. Many parents and caregivers are grieving the loss of life as they once knew it. As the added stressors of having a child with ASD begin to build, family structure can often start to break down, causing families to lose interest in things that used to bring them joy (Walton, 2016; Tint & Weiss, 2016).

Acceptance

It is important to realize that acceptance is not the same as being "OK" with the diagnosis (Kessler, 2018). Often families are never truly at peace with a diagnosis of autism, yet they choose to accept what is in order to move ahead in the best interest of their child (Boushey, 2001). During this phase, parents may still experience episodes from the other four stages, yet they will often reduce in severity (Kessler, 2018).

Learning to accept the diagnosis can encourage parents to become better advocates for their child's needs in addition to learning how to develop a flexible parenting style. It is at this point that parents begin to reach out for support from outside individuals and groups as they begin to feel that they can cope with the diagnosis (Haley et al., 2013). During this phase it is essential for parents to focus on the positives exhibited by their child. This will both help the parent cope better with the diagnosis and will also promote the child's self-esteem and feelings of self-confidence.

FURTHER IMPACTS ON THE FAMILY UNIT

Siblings

It is no surprise that it is not only the parents that are affected by the diagnosis of autism in a family member. Research suggests that typically developing siblings of children with ASD can experience a range of both positive and negative outcomes (Walton, 2016). Studies indicate that siblings of children with ASD are at greater risk of social difficulties than the general population.

There is also research that indicates the opposite is true (Walton, 2016; Walton & Ingersoll, 2015). There are many factors that may influence whether or not siblings of children with ASD experience social challenges. Some studies suggest that the lone siblings of children with ASD have greater support needs, possibly due in part to a lack of inner-family supports (e.g., other siblings) to whom they can go for help (Walton, 2016).

Walton (2016) and Walton and Ingersoll (2015) conducted studies involving siblings of children with autism in order to determine risk factors for social and behavioral difficulties. It was found that lower family income, male gender, and having fewer siblings correlated to higher levels of externalizing behavior on behalf of the sibling (Walton, 2016; Walton & Ingersoll, 2015). This would include behaviors such as outbursts, trouble staying seated, refusal to listen to authority, and the like.

Conversely, Walton and Ingersoll (2015) found that factors such as older age of the child with ASD correlated to increases in siblings' internalizing behavior. This would include depression, anxiety, difficulty making friends, and so forth. Interestingly, they also found that siblings of children with ASD often mimicked their symptoms in social situations, experiencing higher degrees of social challenges than would be generally expected. Walton (2016) concluded that it is possible that the behaviors of the child with ASD put more stress on the siblings, which in turn leads to the siblings exhibiting challenges of their own.

There are positives among relationships between children with autism and their typically developing siblings. An autism diagnosis can actually create a tighter bond between siblings because the typically developed sibling acts as a protector to his or her sibling with ASD. This is most typically seen in females who have a sister with ASD (Walton, 2016). Furthermore, having a sibling with ASD teaches typically developed children about acceptance. Appreciating their autistic sibling's strengths and challenges is critical in maintaining positive feelings regarding the diagnosis (Searing, Graham, & Grainger, 2015).

Marriages

The stress of having an autistic child can also put pressure on marriages. As would likely be expected, parents of children with ASD experience higher levels of emotional distress (Ramisch, 2012). Most often, rifts within the marriage are caused by a feeling that the other spouse misunderstands the child's condition and therefore lacks the knowledge to be supportive. Often, spouses fail to discuss their child's condition, and as a result, they both feel different but equally straining burdens (Neely et al., 2012).

Ramisch (2012) conducted a case study in which possible stressors on marriages and the potential effectiveness of marital therapists are examined. Ramisch (2012) suggests that there are many factors to be considered when analyzing a strained marriage in a family with an autistic child.

It is necessary to examine all of the stressors that existed for the family before the autism diagnosis. More often than not, the autistic child is not the only stressor within the family dynamic (Ramisch, 2012). Obtaining a correct diagnosis for the child is an enormous stressor that causes frustration and anger within family units, especially when one parent is convinced of autism and the other parent is not committed to that diagnosis. Add in the problematic behaviors demonstrated by the child, and it is easy to see why parents are exhausted with the child and each other.

Financial hardship—although it should go without saying—poses another challenge to the marriage. Ramisch (2012) suggests that treatment and specialized child care costs often destabilize the marriage as many times one parent has to act as caregiver while the other takes on extra work hours to provide for the family. This perceived disparity in roles can lead to resentment between spouses (Neely et al., 2012).

The Family Unit as a Whole

Recognizing that families with autistic children will likely experience more substantial challenges than families with typically developing children is critical in providing support to the family structure (Russa, Matthews, & Owen-DeSchryver, 2015; Tint & Weiss, 2016). Research suggests that parents of children with ASD report more stress than parents of typically developed children and children with other forms of developmental disabilities (Russa, Matthews, & Owen-DeSchryver, 2015; Silva & Schalock, 2012; Tint & Weiss, 2016).

Hearing the diagnosis of autism is, of course, stressful in and of itself; however, once the diagnosis of autism has been rendered, parents are faced with new stressors such as obtaining services from both school and community and finding relevant information about their child's diagnosis (Russa, Matthews, & Owen-DeSchryver, 2015). As challenges change over the course of the child's developmental stages, parents are likely to need continually changing services and supports.

Finding appropriate supports that can assist families with the changing needs of an autistic child has been shown to be critical in helping parents and caregivers more successfully cope with their child's needs (Searing, Graham, & Grainger, 2015). For instance, during the initial stage of diagnosis, parents are more likely to need support in managing the emotional impact of the diagnosis, as well as to find out information that will help them make sense of the diagnosis, versus the transition to adulthood stage where parents will need help in working with various community-based services to learn how to increase independence in their child (Russa, Matthews, & Owen-DeSchryver, 2015).

Many of the challenges faced by families of autistic children have to do with the stress of obtaining services for their child. For parents who lack the knowledge of where to find appropriate services or which services are relevant to their child's needs, the stress can become overwhelming (Russa, Matthews, & Owen-DeSchryver, 2015). As families experience the continued burden of figuring out ways in which to navigate the autism landscape without appropriate support, a decreased quality of life and higher levels of dissatisfaction with the situation may occur (Russa, Matthews, & Owen-DeSchryver, 2015).

As many families look to schools to help them with obtaining services, the reality is that schools often fall short in what they can realistically provide or have limited connections to outside community resources. Furthermore, parents often report their dissatisfaction with schools insofar as placement options and assistance with social and communication development (Mereoiu et al., 2015). Even when students are diagnosed early and supports are put into place, parents report the fidelity with which educators employ these supports is spotty at best (Mereoiu et al., 2015).

It is especially important for teachers to recognize their role as a main support for families of students with ASD (Garbacz, McIntyre, & Santiago, 2016). While many families are skeptical of the educational system for myriad reasons including their own experiences in school, it is vital to the autistic child's educational progress to maintain an open collaboration with families and encourage them to become active members in the decision making surrounding their child's education (Garbacz, McIntyre, & Santiago, 2016).

SUPPORTING THE WHOLE FAMILY: STRATEGIES AND RESOURCES

It is clear that a need for consistent, supportive services is necessary to increase the well-being of families with children on the autism spectrum (Tint & Weiss, 2016). Yet, in addition to being uncertain as to where to locate such services, many families are unsure about what these services look like. The following is a sampling of services that have been shown to benefit families of autistic children (Russa, Matthews, & Owen-DeSchryver, 2015).

Positive Behavioral Interventions and Supports (PBIS)

PBIS is an approach that promotes effective behavior intervention through multileveled systems of support (Positive Behavioral Interventions and Supports, 2018). PBIS incorporates positive reinforcement with data collection to make educated decisions about the ways in which to change target behaviors in students or school-wide (Positive Behavioral Interventions and Supports, 2018). Studies have shown that family engagement is associated with better behavioral and academic outcomes (Garbacz, Witte, & Houck, 2017). Behavioral interventions that include assistance from family members contribute substantially to the reduction in disruptive behaviors (Garbacz, Witte, & Houck, 2017).

In order to successfully utilize parental support, PBIS practitioners teach parents the ways to create contexts in which disruptive behaviors are no longer sufficient in gaining a desired outcome (Russa, Matthews, & Owen-DeSchryver, 2015). As a result, employing this type of technique will significantly decrease the stressors on the family insofar as behavior is a concern, as students will begin to respond to the behavior intervention both at home and in the community (Russa, Matthews, & Owen-DeSchryver, 2015).

Parent to Parent (PTP)

PTP is an organization that has nationwide chapters serving to connect parents of children with disabilities with other parents who have similar experiences (Russa, Matthews, & Owen-DeSchryver, 2015; Family Ties of Massachusetts, 2012). PTP works by parents contacting their local chapter and requesting to speak with a parent who shares similar struggles. Once a match is made by program coordinators, parents are able to discuss concerns and request assistance with disability information from their volunteer parent mentor (Family Ties of Massachusetts, 2012). Mentor parents are trained to provide relevant assistance for families who are struggling with initial diagnoses, service obtainment, behavior management strategies, and other aspects of the child's disability (Russa, Matthews, & Owen-DeSchryver, 2015).

Paren–Teacher Collaboration

Effective collaboration between home and school is key to developing the most appropriate education plans for children with ASD; however, as many parents have trust issues with the education system, it can be challenging to ensure that both family and school are on the same page. Enhancing communication with families allows parents to feel as though they are valued members of the team planning process (Garbacz, McIntyre, & Santiago, 2016). Additionally, schools that provide teacher training on meaningful collaboration often see better outcomes when working with parents (Russa, Matthews, & Owen-DeSchryver, 2015).

Several states are beginning to implement programs that train teachers on effective collaboration with parents and families. Teachers who complete these programs become mentors to parents of children with ASD, helping them to understand the IEP process, autism-related topics, and how to become a successful member of the team (Russa, Matthews, & Owen-DeSchryver, 2015). Programs such as the Collaborative Model for Promoting Competence and Success for Students (COMPASS) with ASD have been shown to be beneficial to both parents and educators who wish to develop a better understanding of their roles as well as the most effective ways to work together to improve student outcomes (Ruble et al., 2010).

Family Navigator Programs

Similar to PTP, Family Navigator programs are available in many different locations around the country. The goal of this intervention model is to empower and support families by working collaboratively to help them obtain services for their child (University of Miami Health System, 2018). Family Navigator has the ability to help identify family strengths, connect families with needed services, provide advocacy services for the child, address educational concerns, and provide connections with other parents and families who have experience with raising children with disabilities (Russa, Matthews, & Owen-DeSchryver, 2015; University of Miami Health System, 2018).

Marriage and Family Therapists (MFTs)

MFTs can positively contribute to maintaining the family structure during times of increased stress. Through their unique experience working with families under a variety of stressors, MFTs can help families of children with ASD to navigate through the grieving process as well as begin to come to an understanding of the impact the diagnosis will have on all family members (Neely et al., 2012). MFTs can also provide assistance for families who begin to have difficulties with sibling behavior.

These stressors are interconnected, and seeking family therapy is often a respite in a world of chaos. MFTs can mediate difficult discussions and decision making when a diagnosis of autism has been found (Neely et al., 2012). These therapists have an extensive understanding of the dynamics of the family unit; thus, MFTs have a unique ability to guide families toward interventions and practices that will benefit both the family and the autistic child.

FINAL THOUGHTS

Due to the nature of an autism diagnosis and all the challenges that come with it, families of children with ASD are likely to require intense support to maintain their well-being (Tint & Weiss, 2016). Dealing with an autism diagnosis can evoke feelings of grief in parents, especially mothers, so it is important for families to develop an understanding of the grief process and how to manage it through support. As parents and family members come to terms with the autism diagnosis, they are better able to make informed decisions about their child's treatment options and future outlook (Haley et al., 2013). In addition to the grief they feel over an autism diagnosis, parents are often dealing with the grief of siblings, which can often put a strain on marriages (Ramisch, 2012; Walton, 2016).

With support, the outlook is hopeful for families of children with ASD. Understanding the supports that are available is the first step in deciding upon the best course of intervention for the family unit. It is likely that the family's and child's needs will change throughout the course of the child's development, but being proactive is a necessary step in staying ahead of the increasing challenges (Russa, Matthews, & Owen-DeSchryver, 2015; Searing, Graham, & Grainger, 2015).

Schools should look to become a major source of support for families of autistic children as they are often the best resource for understanding how autism affects children holistically (Garbacz, McIntyre, & Santiago, 2016). Community resources that offer support for children with all types of disabilities can be great places to find others who share similar challenges. Most importantly, families must sustain hope that they are strong enough to face the challenges of autism and create a sustainable and successful future for themselves and their children.

POINTS TO REMEMBER

- *Families who receive a diagnosis of autism for their child are likely to go through the stages of grief including denial, anger, bargaining, depression, and acceptance (Boushey, 2001; Haley et al., 2013).*
- *A diagnosis of autism amounts to feelings of loss for many families, especially when family members feel as though their lives have been forever changed.*
- *Parents are not the only family members affected by a diagnosis of autism; siblings are often affected adversely, manifesting as difficulties with externalizing and internalizing behavior (Walton, 2016; Walton & Ingersoll, 2015).*
- *Marriages can be strained by the perception that spouses misunderstand the child's condition as well as their refusal to talk about the child's condition (Neely et al., 2012).*
- *Additional stressors to families of children with ASD include financial hardship, lack of knowledge of autism, and limited access to support services (Russa, Matthews, & Owen-DeSchryver, 2015; Searing, Graham, & Grainger, 2015).*
- *Supports are available for families of children with ASD. With these supports, the outlook remains positive for maintaining the family structure.*

Chapter Ten

Transition Planning for Autistic Students

Preparing for Postsecondary and Workforce Transitions

The number of students with disabilities, including autism, seeking postsecondary educational opportunities has risen in the last decade (Krupnick, 2014; Vaccaro, Daly-Cano, & Newman, 2015). As a result, institutions of higher education need to be ready to meet the needs of this diverse population of nontraditional students (Young & Jean, 2018). Federal mandates at the postsecondary level outline a modest set of accommodations and services for students with disabilities that colleges and universities are encouraged to extend whenever possible to ensure the success of their students with disabilities (Vaccaro, Daly-Cano, & Newman, 2015; Young & Bonanno-Sotiropoulos, 2018).

Colleges and universities are required to adhere to minimal federal mandates meant to provide reasonable accommodations for students with a documented disability (Young & Jean, 2018). Yet the academic and social demands of college are great, and, according to Longtin (2014), "the success or failure of these students [with disabilities] once enrolled in college could be determined by the degree to which they can be supported by their institution of higher education" (p. 64).

The other piece of the puzzle includes PK–12 education better preparing students with disabilities to be successful in postsecondary settings and/or the workforce. This includes increasing independence, self-awareness, self-advocacy, and self-determination skills (Hong, 2015). Students of the future who have disabilities must be better equipped with the tools and strategies they need to gain full access to an education after high school and/or gainful employment.

Research has highlighted the need for effective transition planning and supports that bridge the gap between secondary and postsecondary environments. Many would even argue that transition planning should occur even earlier than high school (Young & Bonanno-Sotiropoulos, 2018). For many students with disabilities, support in the areas of self-advocacy, self-determination, social skills, independence, and academic assistance is needed (Vaccaro, Daly-Cano, & Newman, 2015; Hong, 2015; Young & Bonanno-Sotiropoulos, 2018).

Relevant literature shows that additional preparation, support, and resources are needed for students with autism (Daly-Cano et al., 2015; Garrison-Wade, 2012). The development of effective transition programs at the secondary level in partnership with support programs at the postsecondary level is vital to student success (Daly-Cano et al., 2015; Garrison-Wade, 2012). Research has proven that the development of self-advocacy skills, self-determination skills, and disability awareness are directly correlated to successful academic, social, and emotional outcomes of students with disabilities (Daly-Cano et al., 2015; Garrison-Wade, 2012).

A COMPARISON OF MANDATES AND SPECIAL EDUCATION SERVICES

Students with disabilities enter college with educational needs similar to when they were in high school; however, they must be more self-directed and self-advocating in managing their learning and gaining access to the postsecondary environment (McCall, 2015). The National Center for Learning Disabilities (Coriella & Horowitz, 2017) reports that a mere 17% of disabled students seek help at the college level. One reason for this low number is that many students with learning disabilities view starting college as a fresh start and attempt to navigate the experience on their own. Another reason is due to underdeveloped or nonexistent self-advocating skills and a lack of understanding of how a disability affects the individual (Young & Bonanno-Sotiropoulos, 2018).

There are three federal regulations that protect the rights of individuals with disabilities—the Individuals with Disabilities Education Act (IDEA), Section 504 of the 1973 Rehabilitation Act, and the Americans with Disabilities Act (Young & Jean, 2018; Social Welfare History Project, 2016). These regulations shield individuals from discrimination based upon their disability and provide for reasonable accommodations and services to assist individuals with disabilities to gain access to the environment, learning, and services.

The IDEA protects children and students from birth to age 21 (Lee, 2016; Social Welfare History Project, 2016). This regulation provides for such things as free and appropriate public education, parent and student involvement, and participation in the least restrictive environment. Section 504 of the 1973 Rehabilitation Act is a civil rights act that ensures an individual's civil rights despite their disability (Zeisler, 2018). Section 504 of the 1973 Rehabilitation Act applies to any school, agency, and institution that receive federal funding and, as such, refusal to follow federal mandates can result in funds being removed (Zeisler, 2018). This regulation also ensures a free and appropriate public education at the PK–12 level, but only provides for accommodations at the postsecondary level (U.S. Department of Labor, n.d.).

Postsecondary education is different in terms of mandates and what institutions are required to provide for students with disabilities (Young & Jean, 2018). According to the U.S. Department of Education (2011b), "postsecondary schools are not required to provide free and appropriate public education [but] are required to provide appropriate academic adjustments as necessary to ensure that it does not discriminate on the basis of disability" (p. 2). Postsecondary schools that receive federal funding must abide by the regulations outlined in Section 504 of the 1973 Rehabilitation Act as well as Title II of the Americans with Disabilities Act (Young & Jean, 2018; Zeisler, 2018).

Title II of the Americans with Disabilities Act requires "public colleges, universities, and graduate and professional schools . . . the provision of auxiliary aids and services" (U.S. Department of Education, 1998, p. 2). Auxiliary aids include such things as audio texts, interpreters, electronic readers, closed captioning, assistive listening devices, and note-takers. These types of aids are similar to those provided in PK–12 settings; however, it is important to note that colleges have the "flexibility in choosing the specific aid or service it provides to the student, as long as the aid or service is useful" (U.S. Department of Education, 1998, p. 3).

Under these regulations, higher education institutions are not required to provide devices or services of a personal nature. This means that all devices are to be used within the classroom or campus setting only and not for personal use, such as a method of studying. Auxiliary aids and services do not include personal aids or attendants, similar to paraprofessionals in an elementary or secondary school setting (Young & Bonanno-Sotiropoulos, 2018).

The language in the regulation explicitly states that "recipients [colleges and universities] need not provide attendants, individually prescribed devices, readers for personal use or study, or other devices or services of a personal nature" (U.S. Department of Education, 1998, p. 5). It is difficult to understand the reasoning behind a restriction placed on using a human reader or an auxiliary device for studying.

Students receiving special education services in PK–12 settings differ drastically from services offered at the postsecondary level (Young & Bonanno-Sotiropoulos, 2018). Before the age of 14, planning and decision making is a collaborative effort between the parents and school personnel, with little or no input from the student. It is not until the student reaches the age of 14, or older in most cases, that most students become aware of having an individual education plan (IEP), let alone having a disability.

Students with disabilities, therefore, enter college with needs similar to when they were in high school, except now they must become self-directed in managing their learning and gaining access to the postsecondary environment (Hong, 2015; Young & Bonanno-Sotiropoulos, 2018). Students with disabilities accomplish this through a deeper understanding of how their disability affects learning and identification of the supports they need to be successful.

Unlike PK–12, when a student enters the world of postsecondary education, the supports they may have been used to are no longer provided. Supports, such as specialized instruction and modifications to content, no longer exist. It now becomes the student's full responsibility to advocate for him- or herself, such as identifying as having a disability, requesting appropriate accommodations and services, and reporting this information to the appropriate office within the college (U.S. Department of Education, 2011a; Young & Bonanno-Sotiropoulos, 2018).

GETTING TO KNOW THE POSTSECONDARY STUDENT WITH DISABILITIES

For individuals with disabilities to be effective in postsecondary settings, faculty and staff must understand how disabilities may affect the learning process as well as social development. Access to resources that help assist in accommodating students through teaching and learning is another key component. Faculty must be aware of the impact that they have on students with disabilities and must be able to provide equality at all times (Young & Jean, 2018). It is the responsibility of the university to provide training, resources, and ongoing support to ensure that equality is the norm (Marquis et al., 2016; Padden & Ellis, 2015; Young & Jean, 2018).

Postsecondary institutions should provide faculty, and possibly students, with ongoing professional development focusing on awareness, legal mandates, differentiation, and sensitivity training (Picard, 2015; Young & Jean, 2018). An attitudinal barrier, or the belief that some professors hold negative attitudes toward students with disabilities and their right to accommodations and services, may pose an unexpected challenge as well (Garrison-Wade, 2012). Providing open lectures, documentary screenings, collaborative trainings, handouts and reference sheets, and access to additional faculty resources, as well as student trainings about disabilities, would be just a few ways to bring awareness and acceptance to college campuses (Padden & Ellis, 2015).

Garrison-Wade (2012) conducted a study with 59 students with disabilities focused on factors that impact success in college. Interestingly, three reoccurring themes surfaced from this research that warrant consideration including (1) capitalizing on student self-determination skills, (2) implementing formalized planning processes, and (3) improving postsecondary support. Capitalizing on student self-determination skills requires "creating high expectations," which helps to "influence students' perceptions about their capabilities" (Garrison-Wade, 2012, p. 117). Postsecondary instructors can accomplish this by gaining awareness about the various types of disabilities and how to support their students both in and out of class.

It is imperative that faculty know, understand, and comply with the legal mandates of providing accommodations to ensure the successful journey for these students, although perhaps more importantly, faculty must know how to effectively differentiate instruction, assignments, and assessments as well (Picard, 2015; Young & Jean, 2018). This will benefit students with disabilities and also accommodate different learning styles, interests, and cultural experiences of all students.

AUTISM IN POSTSECONDARY EDUCATION

The number of students diagnosed with autism who are attending postsecondary institutions has been increasing over the past few decades. Most students with ASD have the intellectual capability to succeed in college, they simply learn differently; however, it is the psychosocial challenges that prove to be the most difficult as they have

> difficulty engaging in reciprocal social interactions and relationship development, problems maintaining a conversation in social settings, perseverative obsessive thought patterns, fixated or restricted behaviors or interests, and difficulty interpreting nonverbal cues or the perspectives of others. (Pinder-Amaker, 2014, p. 125)

Because of these social challenges, students with ASD have an increased risk for difficult postsecondary experiences.

Similar to Pinder-Amaker (2014), Longtin (2014) reiterates that students with autism and other disabilities struggle with social issues, which can result in "difficulty interacting with professors and classmates [which ultimately may lead to] academic problems" (p. 65). Furthermore, students with autism and other disabilities may struggle with "executive function skills [such as] planning, flexibility, self-monitoring, working memory, and goal setting, which contribute to difficulty in learning and successful independence" (Longtin, 2014, p. 65).

In addition to the other skills mentioned previously, it is important to teach these critical skills to students before they enter postsecondary settings and then provide ongoing support to maintain these skills in postsecondary settings. Skills such as self-monitoring and goal-setting should be goals written into students' individual education plans from the very start. Teaching self-monitoring and goal-setting skills are becoming more common in the classroom at all levels, particularly in the realm of special education, which is especially promising (Young & Bonanno-Sotiropoulos, 2018).

Much has been written about the correlation between stress and increased anxiety and depression for individuals with ASD (Longtin, 2014; Pinder-Amaker, 2014; Young & Bonanno-Sotiropoulos, 2018). The need for smooth transitions, including the development of self-determination and self-advocacy skills, is critical to the success of this population after the completion of secondary schooling. Successful coordination between high schools and postsecondary schools must be explored and further developed. Some of the problems students with ASD experience when transitioning to college include increased stress over academic achievement, developing and maintaining relationships, and living away from home (Hong, 2015, Pinder-Amaker, 2014).

There are several ways that both secondary and postsecondary schools can provide the support and guidance for students with ASD to achieve successful outcomes. To help ensure smooth transitions and supports for students with disabilities—specifically autism—include building self-advocacy skills before entering postsecondary settings, ensuring that the principles of Universal Design for Learning are embedded in courses throughout postsecondary institutions, access to tutoring centers and counseling centers, and even providing summer bridge programs and support groups for students with disabilities entering into postsecondary settings (Longtin, 2015; Pinder-Amaker, 2014; CAST, 2018).

PLANNING FOR TRANSITION

Longtin (2014) suggests that "secondary schools could help ensure that their students on the spectrum [or other disabilities] who wish to go to college have the readiness skills to enroll by providing advanced preparation in the social, self-advocacy, and organizational domains during the IDEA mandated transition-planning phase of high school" (Longtin, 2014, p. 64). The IDEA recommends transition planning to include preparation for college, career, and the skills needed to obtain these goals. The transition planning starts at age 14 so that middle schools and high schools can provide the necessary services, preparation, and training for students so that they experience successful transitions into college and careers (Young & Bonanno-Sotiropoulos, 2018).

Self-Advocacy Skills

Skinner (1998) believes that the most important skill that students with disabilities need to learn before attending postsecondary schooling is self-advocacy. Skinner defines self-advocacy skills as the ability to recognize and meet the needs of one's disability, have an understanding of one's disability, and practice competent communication skills when advocating for oneself (Skinner, 1998; Young & Bonanno-Sotiropoulos, 2018).

Understanding individual strengths and weaknesses, as well as their rights under federal laws, allows people with disabilities to have a better grasp of what they need in terms of accommodations and services in order to be successful. In addition, the ability to effectively communicate is necessary to ensure awareness as to what supports are vital for individuals (Young & Bonanno-Sotiropoulos, 2018).

There continues to be a lack of preparation for these skills in high schools for students with all types of disabilities including autism (Pinder-Amaker, 2014; Longtin, 2014; Skinner, 1998). Not only do these skills need to be taught, reinforced, and supported in the PK–12 setting, but also these skills need to be followed up on at the postsecondary level. Some ways that colleges can support these skills and behaviors is through the use of counseling centers, disability resource centers, student support centers, and support groups (Skinner, 1998; Young & Bonanno-Sotiropoulos, 2018).

Gregg (2007) supports the message that secondary educators need to have transitional programs in place that focus on all areas of college preparation including the development of self-advocacy skills, knowledge of the student's rights under federal regulations, and how to navigate the postsecondary environment to ensure appropriate supports and services are accessible. Further, Gregg (2007) suggests that establishing partnerships between secondary schools and postsecondary institutions would be an effective way to help prepare students with disabilities proactively navigate the postsecondary environment.

Hadley (2011) supports the research and reiterates that college students with disabilities must "successfully self-advocate . . . [and] have a good understanding of their particular disability and the compensatory strategies that work best for them" (p. 78). Going to college is a difficult transition for students with disabilities, they may be unaware of the academic challenges and the social changes unique to the college experience.

Hadley (2011) supports the ideas set forth by both Skinner (1998) and Gregg (2007) acknowledging that postsecondary institutions need to do a better job assisting students with disabilities in further developing their independence, self-determination, and self-advocacy skills. We must acknowledge that students with disabilities might not fully understand or experience the effects of their disability immediately upon entering postsecondary education. Rather, transition should be viewed as a process that requires ongoing support.

Prater et al. (2014) support the research and acknowledge the importance of self-advocacy skills, which allow individuals to fully understand how their disability affects various aspects of their lives. Through self-advocacy, individuals are able to identify their personal strengths and weaknesses, request accommodations and services needed to be successful, and gain access to the learning environment as well as understand their rights under the law. The importance of teaching and developing self-advocacy skills throughout a student's educational career cannot be overlooked, as this will ensure better transition into the real world (Young & Bonanno-Sotiropoulos, 2018).

Self-Determination Skills

Vaccaro, Daly-Cano, and Newman (2015) examined the connection between a sense of belonging and an increase in academic motivation, success, and persistence. These characteristics contribute to what is referred to as "self-determination." According to researchers, a sense of belonging encompasses the feeling of being a part of a community or group, including having access to a built-in support system (Young & Bonanno-Sotiropoulos, 2018).

The playing field changes as students enter the postsecondary setting; specifically, taking on the role of decision maker, where the individual with a disability must navigate the world of self-advocacy, necessary accommodations, and support services by and for themselves. It is believed that if students feel a sense of belonging, they will have a better chance of accessing those support systems and acquire the services they need (Vaccaro, Daly-Cano, & Newman, 2015).

Vaccaro, Daly-Cano, and Newman (2015) dive deeper into the theory of self-advocacy and reveal some key components. Knowledge of an individual's rights, disability, strengths, and weaknesses, as well as learning style, are all important pieces of becoming a self-advocating individual. For students in postsecondary settings, as part of self-advocating, students must seek assistance through disability centers, support services, and building relationships with professors and peers. By engaging in these proactive strategies, students are developing a sense of belonging within the college community.

Evans Getzel (2014) looks at self-determination and self-advocacy skills and their correlation to postsecondary attendance and academic success.

Self-determination refers to the ability to achieve goals by understanding an individual's strengths and identifying an individual's needs. Evans Getzel (2014) supports the argument of the importance of developing self-determination and self-advocacy skills, by citing the increase in postsecondary attendance and positive academic and social outcomes in postsecondary settings.

EFFECTIVE TRANSITION POSTSECONDARY SUPPORTS AND SERVICES

Many students come to the college campus with an IEP or 504 from a public secondary institution. It is then incumbent upon the postsecondary institution to create an individualized success plan as IEPs and 504s are not binding documents at the postsecondary level, although institutions are federally mandated to provide equal access and reasonable accommodations (IDEA, 2006; Young & Jean, 2018). Colleges and universities must first decide what that means to that particular institution and then what it means for their student body. The college must also assist the student in finding the proper supports and implementing them, being helpful not just to the student, but also to the professor (Young & Jean, 2018). Accommodations such as extended test time, interpreters, and certain technologies would qualify; however, if more detailed and in-depth supports are required, it is up to the disability office to also come up with a plan for these students (Young & Jean, 2018).

With a student success plan clearly in place—one that properly matches effective interventions related to the disability and identified academic challenges—there is a far better chance for a successful postsecondary outcome (Grigal, Hart, & Weir, 2013; Young & Bonanno-Sotiropoulos, 2018). A more in-depth plan such as an individualized plan of study could also be developed. An individualized plan of study would go a step further and identify the specific goals a student needs to achieve while attending college, such as career goals, self-determination skills, and life planning skills (Miller et al., 2016; Young & Bonanno-Sotiropoulos, 2018).

The Intent of Postsecondary Service Centers

In order for students with learning disabilities to be successful once enrolled, the respective higher education institution must take an active role in providing supports, accommodations, and a conducive environment for learning (Garrison-Wade, 2012; Longtin, 2014; Young & Jean, 2018). To this end, colleges are encouraged to establish disability centers that cater to the needs of their students and support them throughout their academic career. College disability service centers can also provide ongoing professional development and online information for easy access for faculty, while instructors should take the initiative to learn more about the various types of disabilities and how to make the necessary accommodations for them (Marquis et al., 2016; Young & Jean, 2018; Picard, 2015).

Postsecondary institutions should consider incorporating more proactive means such as integrating principles of Universal Design for Learning throughout the campus and in classrooms, while creating and supporting meaningful connections with students are crucial (CAST, 2018; Picard, 2015; Young & Jean, 2018). Additionally, having access to peer mentors, counselors, and peer support groups can provide the ongoing encouragement needed to maintain student success (Hadley, 2011; Griffin et al., 2016). These are some important features of a disability-friendly campus landscape (Young & Jean, 2018).

Capitalizing on student self-determination skills requires "creating high expectations," which helps to "influence students' perceptions about their capabilities" (Garrison-Wade, 2012, p. 117). Postsecondary instructors can accomplish this by gaining awareness about the various types of disabilities and how to support their students both in and out of class. It is imperative that faculty know, understand, and comply with the legal mandates of providing accommodations to ensure the successful journey for these students (Young & Jean, 2018).

Although knowing and understanding the legal mandates is a great start, faculty must know how to effectively differentiate instruction, assignments, and assessments as well. This not only will help students with disabilities, but also accommodate for different learning styles, interests, and cultural experiences (Celli & Young, 2014). Implementing a formalized planning process requires that high schools do a better job at preparing students with disabilities for a successful transition into postsecondary settings.

The preparation process should include exposure to such things as how high school environments and supports are different from college environments and supports. Students should know what to expect regarding levels of support. Students should have knowledge of how to request accommodations and services and where help can be found within the college campus (Young & Bonanno-Sotiropoulos, 2018). Students must also understand how their disability affects them personally and what they need to access the content and environment to be successful.

Improving postsecondary supports for students with disabilities entails advancements in use of accommodations, disability awareness, environmental accessibility, and financial assistance. Specifically looking at disability awareness and the use of accommodations, students in the study felt very challenged with what Garrison-Wade (2012) refers to as "attitudinal barriers [which suggests that] some postsecondary faculty had negative attitudes toward students with disabilities and lacked understanding of their needs and their rights to special accommodations and other supportive services" (p.

121). To address any matters of attitudinal barriers, postsecondary schools must actively fight against this form of discrimination.

Postsecondary institutions should provide faculty with ongoing professional development focusing on awareness, legal mandates, differentiation, and sensitivity training. Training should also extend to the student population as well. Providing open lectures, documentary screenings, and student trainings about disabilities would address the issues and bring awareness and acceptance to college campuses (Young & Jean, 2018).

Finally, the most surprising information that came out of the Garrison-Wade (2012) study was that students with disabilities felt that "their high school classes were not challenging and did little to prepare them for college" (p. 119). This finding speaks directly to the larger problem stated previously by Gregg (2007), who identified the epidemic of lowered academic expectations and the lack of rigorous learning opportunities in PK–12 settings for students who have a learning disability, which was eliminated through the Every Student Succeeds Act, yet continues today due to a lack of educator training (Young & Bonanno-Sotiropoulos, 2018).

The Role of Postsecondary Disability Centers

College campuses that value students with learning disabilities will find a disability center dedicated to the needs of the student. Although students often refuse help at first in an effort to be independent, they soon realize it would be more beneficial to receive assistance than give up and leave school (Krupnick, 2014). Research shows that students who access help from disability centers are more likely to be successful and complete their education (Coriella & Horowitz, 2014; Young & Jean, 2018). While the Americans with Disabilities Act mandates that every postsecondary institution has a disability office, many are understaffed or difficult to find on campus (Young & Jean, 2018). Walker (2016) established the idea of a more inclusive disability and academic success center on postsecondary campuses. When such centers are inclusive to all students with and without disabilities, services offered are less likely to carry a stigma and more likely to be accessed as part of the normal course of taking classes and advancing forward academically at the respective institution by the larger student body (Krupnick, 2014). Academic assistance in such circumstances becomes commonplace and a traditional part of campus life—this is the goal of programming for students with disabilities at all grades and stages.

Adding to the difficulty for students is that often the disability office will require documentation that the student may not have (Young & Jean, 2018). Students who have well-written transition plans in secondary school, or who were willing to self-advocate, fare better in these situations (Krupnick, 2014). Some may find that they need formal diagnostic testing and a documented educational disability to receive academic assistance, which is traditionally something that colleges do not pay for or even offer (Krupnick, 2014).

The fees for testing are on top of regular tuition, and sometimes the disabilities office itself charges for its services due to budgetary considerations. In 2013, for example, the Jones Learning Center, associated with the University of the Ozarks in Clarksville, Arkansas, charged almost as much for their services as they did for tuition; however, some campuses have become creative and even offer specialized programs and/or grant funding to help defray assessment-related expenses (Krupnick, 2014).

Students who make their way to the disabilities office may find a staff member waiting to help. From testing to diagnosis, to accommodations to tutoring, these offices offer a plethora of services to help a student with learning disabilities; for example, a student who is tested and found to have ADHD and dyslexia may be offered special text to speech software (Pierce, 2014). A student who has trouble with writing may need speech to text software, while a student who has trouble with executive functioning may find it helpful to have a tutor to provide organization support.

Not only will these services enhance the understanding of material, but also may keep the student on task, which will lead to increased academic success. At Taft College in Taft, California, an "access specialist" shows students all the possible technologies and learning aids available and it is up to the student to choose what is right for them; students are encouraged to try a varied approach until they find the correct mix of supports (Pierce, 2014).

A subsidiary of the disabilities office may include a coordination and collaboration facilitator whose job it is to connect with outside agencies and organizations. Providing these strategic partnerships ensures an additional layer of help for students with disabilities, maximizes limited funding, and supports the longevity of the programs (Grigal, Hart, & Weir, 2013).

These programs work with existing systems such as the financial aid office, student affairs office, and the registrar and "have a similar positive impact on the effectiveness and sustainability of the program" (Grigal, Hart, & Weir, 2013, p. 56). These programs help with a variety of services for students and families that the postsecondary institution could not do alone; thus, a more balanced palette of services is created.

Effective Transition Planning

Effective transition planning to support the transferal of decision making to the individual with disabilities at the postsecondary level is essential to both academic and social success (Newman, Madaus, & Javitz, 2016). Transition planning must include such components as disability awareness including identification of individual accommodations and effects on academic and social interaction and self-advocacy skills (Newman, Madaus, & Javitz, 2016). Current research revealed that students who received extensive transition planning in high school and engaged in rigorous high school learning experiences were at a higher rate for self-identifying a disability within the postsecondary setting as well as self-advocating for appropriate accommodations (Newman, Madaus, & Javitz, 2016).

Gothberg et al. (2015) suggest that transition planning falls under the services portion of the IDEA and that it is transition services that best prepare students with disabilities for postsecondary education and employment opportunities. As transition planning services are identified under the IDEA, it is reasonable for secondary schools to initiate the transition process and be sure that students are fully ready to transition to college or career.

Gothberg et al. (2015) describe how to write appropriate transition goals. First, IEP teams must identify appropriate postsecondary goal(s) and recognize the skills needed to obtain the postsecondary goal. Once the goal and needed skills are ascertained, the team can connect the student's current performance level to the outcome and plan the steps toward goal achievement (Gothberg et al., 2015).

Connor (2012) identifies 21 transition strategies to increase positive outcomes for students with disabilities. Strategies include having an awareness of the disability and how it affects the individual. Students must know their strengths and weaknesses and most of all what they need to be successful academically, socially, and emotionally (Connor, 2012). Students must be aware of the services, supports, and resources available to them in the postsecondary setting and how to seek them out. Students need opportunities to practice decision-making skills prior to transitioning to postsecondary settings (Connor, 2012).

Connor (2012) recommends that students with disabilities take a college course while in high school. This can be accomplished through partnerships with local colleges. By doing this, students can get a feel for how different the workload may be. In addition to taking a college course, it is recommended that students with disabilities visit and participate in college bridge programs or camps (Woodcock & Olson Beal, 2013). This provides the students with exposure to the environment and a chance to tour the campus and become familiar with the various offices and personnel.

Once at a postsecondary school, students with disabilities should utilize peer tutoring and mentoring (Strayhorn, 2016). Good practices include disability centers pairing students with a mentor who has the same or a similar disability, as this has proven to be valuable both academically and socially. When it comes to courses, students with disabilities should take advantage of the available assistive technology, such as digital recorders, podcasts, time management software, and word processing software. The use of assistive technology can help a student with disabilities stay organized and assist with accessing and understanding the content (Connor, 2012).

Better preparation programs at the secondary level help students to address and develop self-advocacy skills. Students with disabilities in secondary schools have most likely been receiving special education services for several years; however, decision making, advocacy, and legal protections were different than what is provided for at the postsecondary level. Students with disabilities must learn and understand how their disability affects them, what they need, in terms of support, to access learning and be successful and, most importantly, how to become advocates for themselves. This was lacking in many secondary preparation programs.

Hamblet (2014) identifies several ways that secondary IEP team members can start the process of preparing students with disabilities for transitioning. IEP team members, especially at the secondary level, must be familiar with the differences between services and decision making at the secondary level and the postsecondary level. IEP team members, including families, should be educated in the available services, access to these services, and available accommodations at the secondary level. This knowledge can be gained through partnerships with local colleges. College personnel can provide information sessions or professional development for secondary special education teams and families to help facilitate this transfer of knowledge.

IEP teams at the secondary level should practice the reduction of accommodations and modifications for students with disabilities while in high school (Shek & Wong, 2011). This will allow students to experience what it will be like in college and, therefore, provide opportunities for secondary teachers to explicitly teach independence skills. Instead of providing students with study guides, teachers can teach students how to make their own study guides. If students are typically given extra time to complete assignments, this is a good opportunity to teach time management skills (Hamblet, 2014).

In addition, Hamblet (2014) suggests that secondary schools provide current documentation of a disability to students to take with them to postsecondary settings. To accomplish this, students in secondary settings should be reevaluated, including up-to-date academic and psychological testing during the middle to end of high school. By doing this, current information regarding academic knowledge can be obtained and appropriate accommodations can be determined by the IEP team and then transition with the student to postsecondary settings.

Higher education institutions must do a better job at bringing awareness and sensitivity to their campuses and in their classrooms. This can be accomplished with ongoing professional development and resources for faculty. Monthly faculty training, online course modules and resources, collaborative practices, and reimbursement or incentives for training or coursework that occur outside the institution are other examples that higher education institutions should embrace (Young & Jean, 2018).

Postsecondary institutions must ramp up the services and supports that may already be in place for students with disabilities. Some of the recommendations include the use of disability centers to help support the advocacy of students, learning centers to assist with tutoring and study habits, and counseling centers to provide individual counseling and peer support groups (Marshak et al., 2010). One other way that postsecondary institutions can support the success of students with disabilities is to provide peer mentors to assist with the transition process.

POSTSECONDARY SUSTAINABILITY AND EVALUATION OF SUPPORTS FOR STUDENTS WITH DISABILITIES

As part of ensuring quality and responsive service delivery for students with learning disabilities, higher education institutions are encouraged to develop a system for regularly collecting and analyzing data with the goal of constantly improving student outcomes (Joshi & Bouck, 2015). The data should come from a variety of stakeholders including but not limited to families, faculty and administration, and especially students with and without disabilities (Grigal, Hart, & Weir, 2013).

Evidence collected should coordinate with the institutional needs but, at a minimum, look at "student satisfaction, exit and follow-up data . . . perspectives on the program; and family satisfaction with the program" (Grigal, Hart, & Weir, 2013, p. 57). Administration and staff, along with a team of personnel and interested parties, should regularly review the data and make corrections, substitutions, and additions to programs, accommodations, and teaching methods as a way to improve the experience of the student (Young & Boanno-Sotiropoulos, 2018).

This in turn improves the end of course evaluation which "strengthens program longevity [and aids in] securing foundation funding" (Grigal, Hart, & Weir, 2013, p. 57). An evaluation tool that assesses the course and college from a variety of perspectives is likely to lead to a program that is sustainable over a lengthy period of time (Young & Bonanno-Sotiropoulos, 2018).

Staff Training

Postsecondary institutions should be ensuring that they do more than just comply with the federal and state mandates to guarantee accessibility and success for students with disabilities (Young & Bonanno-Sotiropoulos, 2018). It becomes incumbent on institutions to find specific and meaningful ways to support such students. Improving postsecondary supports for students with disabilities entails advancements in use of accommodations, disability awareness, environmental accessibility, and faculty training (Young & Jean, 2018). Multisensory approaches to teaching, including the application of Universal Design for Learning principles and an inclusive classroom, have proven effective for a wide variety of diverse students; however, these are rarely seen at the postsecondary level (CAST, 2018; Marquis et al., 2016; Spencer, 2011).

FINAL THOUGHTS

The literature shows that in order for students with disabilities to be successful in postsecondary institutions there are several key elements that must be in place (Daly-Cano et al., 2015; Hong, 2015; Longtin, 2014; Young & Bonanno-Sotiropoulos, 2018; Young & Jean, 2018). First, the transition from secondary to postsecondary settings must be smooth. This can be accomplished by ensuring that certain preparations take place and partnerships are formed.

Next, secondary schools need to teach students how to be advocates for themselves. Students need to understand their individual strengths and weaknesses associated with their disability. With that understanding comes the identification of what they need regarding accommodations and services to be successful and have access to learning and the environment (Young & Bonanno-Sotiropoulos, 2018).

Then, at the secondary level, the continuation of transition services and supports are critical. Transition supports should include the advanced development of self-advocacy skills, self-determination skills, and an increase in student independence (Young & Bonanno-Sotiropoulos, 2018). Disability awareness is another important component of an effective transition program. Students must understand how their disability affects their learning, social skills development, and access to the environment (Longtin, 2014). In addition, a beneficial transition program addresses the acknowledgement and understanding of an individual's rights under relevant federal and state regulations (Young & Jean, 2018; Lee, 2016).

In regard to postsecondary institutions, there needs to be proactive practices centered around training and supporting faculty in the areas of how they can effectively support students with disabilities in the classroom (Garrison-Wade, 2012; Young & Jean, 2018). Higher education should be providing professional development, support, and resources to their faculty (Garrison-Wade, 2012). By doing this, institutions are arming their faculty with the necessary skills and resources to effectively differentiate within their classrooms (Young & Bonanno-Sotiropoulos, 2018; Young & Jean, 2018).

Last, opportunities to create or expand existing supports for students with disabilities should be high on the priority list for postsecondary institutions.

The number of students attending postsecondary schools is increasing every year (Krupnick, 2014). Higher education institutions need to be ready to support the unique learning needs that come with various types of disabilities. Institutions of higher learning should be offering academic supports, but also mentoring supports, counseling supports, and advocating supports to students with disabilities.

POINTS TO REMEMBER

- *IEPs and 504s do not transfer with the student to the postsecondary level. Institutions are only mandated to make minimal adjustments; therefore, it is necessary for the disability office to create a student success plan that includes accommodations and supports to meet student needs and share it with the faculty.*
- *Students with disabilities, including autism, face a stressful and difficult transition into the postsecondary setting due to challenges with academics, social relationships, and increased independence; however, with the right supports and time, these individuals can achieve academic success they might not have thought possible.*
- *Research has highlighted the need for secondary schools to provide increased transitioning planning, services, and supports. Specifically, instruction and strategies around increasing self-determination and self-advocacy skills are critical to the success of students with disabilities in a postsecondary and/or work environment.*

References

Adams, R. E., Fredstrom, B. K., Duncan, A. W., Holleb, L. J., and Bishop, S. L. (2014). "Using self- and parent-reports to test the association between peer victimization and internalizing symptoms in verbally fluent adolescents with ASD." *Journal of Autism and Developmental Disorders, 44*(4), 861–72. http://dx.doi.org/10.1007/s10803-013-1938-0.

Afach, S. A., Kiwan, E., and Semaan, C. (2018). "How to enhance awareness on bullying for special needs students using 'Edpuzzle' a web 2.0 tool." *International Journal of Educational Research Review, 3*(1), 1–7. Retrieved from https://files.eric.ed.gov/fulltext/ED580839.pdf.

Allred, K. W. (2015). "Engaging parents of students with disabilities: Moving beyond the grief model." *Improving Schools, 18*(1), 46–55. http://dx.doi.org/10.1177/1365480214553745.

Alsubaie, M. A. (2015). "Hidden curriculum as one of current issue of curriculum." *Journal of Education and Practice.* Retrieved from https://files.eric.ed.gov/fulltext/EJ1083566.pdf.

American Occupational Therapy Association. (2018). "Living with an autism spectrum disorder: The high school years." Retrieved from https://www.aota.org/About-Occupational-Therapy/Patients-Clients/ChildrenAndYouth/Autism/ASD-High-School.aspx.

American Psychiatric Association. (1985). *Diagnostic and Statistical Manual of Mental Disorders* (3rd ed.). Washington, DC: American Psychiatric Association.

American Psychiatric Association. (1994). *Diagnostic and Statistical Manual of Mental Disorders* (4th ed.). Washington, DC: American Psychiatric Association.

American Psychiatric Association. (2017). *Diagnostic and Statistical Manual of Mental Disorders* (5th ed.). Washington, DC: American Psychiatric Association.

American Speech-Language-Hearing Association. (2018). "Autism." Retrieved from https://www.asha.org/PRPSpecificTopic.aspx?folderid=8589935303&section=Causes.

Anglim, J., Prendeville, P., and Kinsella, W. (2017). "The self-efficacy of primary teachers in supporting the inclusion of children with autism spectrum disorder." *Educational Psychology in Practice, 34*(1), 73–88. http://dx.doi.org/10.1080/02667363.2017.1391750.

Anson, H. M., Todd, J. T., and Cassaretto, K. J. (2008). "Replacing overt verbal and gestural prompts with unobtrusive covert tactile prompting for students with autism." *Behavior Research Methods, 40*(4), 1106–10. http://dx.doi.org/10.3758/BRM.40.4.1106.

Asaro-Saddler, K., Muir Knox, H., Meredith, H., and Akhmedjanova, D. (2015). "Using technology to support students with autism spectrum disorders in the writing process: A pilot study." *Insights into Learning Disabilities, 12*(2), 103–19. Retrieved from https://files.eric.ed.gov/fulltext/EJ1088270.pdf.

Associated Press. (2017). "Innovative housing options help autistic adults find independence." Retrieved from https://www.statnews.com/2017/04/08/autism-adults-housing/.

Astington, J. W., and Edward, M. J. (2010). "The development of theory of mind in early childhood." In R. E. Tremblay, M. Boivin, R. DeV. Peters, P. D. Zelazo, eds. *Encyclopedia on Early Childhood Development* [online]. Retrieved from http://www.child-encyclopedia.com/social-cognition/according-experts/development-theory-mind-early-childhood.

Austin, K. (2011). "Teaching social skills through social narratives: Another evidence-based practice." Innovations and Perspectives, VCU Virginia Department of Education's Training & Technical Assistance Center. Retrieved from http://www.ttacnews.vcu.edu/2011/09/teaching-social-skills-through-social-narratives-another-evidence-based-practice/.

Autism Science Foundation. (2018). "Our mission." Retrieved from https://autismsciencefoundation.org/about-asf/our-mission/.

Autism Society (2015). "Causes." Retrieved from http://www.autism-society.org/what-is/causes/.

Autism Society. (2016a). "Medical diagnosis." Retrieved from http://www.autism-society.org/what-is/diagnosis/medical-diagosis/.

Autism Society (2016b). "What is autism?" Retrieved from http://www.autism-society.org/what-is/.

Autism Society. (2016c). "Signs and symptoms." Retrieved from http://www.autism-society.org/what-is/symptoms/.

Autism Society of North Carolina. (2018). "Executive summary strategic plan 2017–2020." Retrieved from https://www.autismsociety-nc.org/wp-content/uploads/2017-20-Exec.-Summary_r2.pdf.

Autism Speaks. (2010). "Autism Speaks again calls upon the federal government to increase funding for autism." Retrieved from https://www.autismspeaks.org/about-us/press-releases/autism-speaks-again-calls-upon-federal-government-increase-funding-autism.

Autism Speaks (2012). "Supporting learning in the student with autism." Retrieved from https://www.autismspeaks.org/sites/default/files/sctk_supporting_learning.pdf.

Autism Speaks. (2018a). "Glossary of terms." Retrieved from https://www.autismspeaks.org/what-autism/video-glossary/glossary-terms.

Autism Speaks (2018b). "Learn the signs of autism." Retrieved from https://www.autismspeaks.org/what-autism/learn-signs.

Autism Speaks. (2018c). "Applied behavior analysis." Retrieved from https://www.autismspeaks.org/what-autism/treatment/applied-behavior-analysis-aba.

Autism Speaks. (2018d). "Augmentation of CA CADDRE studies." Retrieved from https://www.autismspeaks.org/science/grants/augmentation-ca-caddre-studies.

Autism Speaks. (2018e). "About us." Retrieved from https://www.autismspeaks.org/about-us.

Autism Speaks. (2018f). "ABLE–The Achieving a Better Life Experience Act." Retrieved from https://www.autismspeaks.org/advocacy/federal/able.

Autism Speaks. (2018g). "What treatments are available for speech, language, and motor issues?" Retrieved from https://www.autismspeaks.org/what-autism/treatment/what-treatments-are-available-speech-language-and-motor-impairments.

Autism Speaks. (2018h). "Treatments & therapies." Retrieved from https://www.autismspeaks.org/family-services/tool-kits/100-day-kit/treatments-therapies.

Azad, G. F., Locke, J., Downey, M. M., Xie, M., and Mandell, D. S. (2015). "One-to-one assistant engagement in autism support classrooms." *Teacher Education and Special Education, 38*(4), 337–46. http://dx.doi.org/10.1177/0888406415603208.

Baker, J. (2005). "Social skills training for students with ASD and their peers." *Organization for Autism Research*. Retrieved from https://researchautism.org/social-skills-training-for-students-with-asd-and-their-peers/.

Bal, V. H., Kim, S., Cheong, D., and Lord, C. (2015). "Daily living skills in individuals with autism spectrum disorder from 2 to 21 years of age." *Autism, 19*(7), 774–84. http://dx.doi.org/10.1177/1362361315575840.

Baron-Cohen, S., Lombardo, M. V., Auyeung, B., Ashwin, E., Chakrabarti, B., and Knickmeyer, R. (2011). "Why are autism spectrum conditions more prevalent in males?" *Public Library of Science Biology, 9*(6), 1–10. http://dx.doi.org/10.1371/journal.pbio.1001081.

Behavioral Dynamics (2018). "About the MotivAider." Retrieved from http://habitchange.com/motivaider.php.

References

Bleicher, A. (2013). "Hunting for autism's earliest clues." Retrieved from https://www.autismspeaks.org/science/science-news/hunting-autisms-earliest-clues.

Boardman, A. G., Arguelles, M. E., Vaughn, S., Hughes, M. T., and Klinger, J. (2005). "Special education teachers' views of research-based practices." *The Journal of Special Education, 39*(3), 168–80. http://dx.doi.org/10.1177/00224669050390030401.

Boshoff, K., and Stewart, H. (2013). "Key principles for confronting the challenges of collaboration in educational settings." *Australian Occupational Therapy Journal, 60*(2), 144–47. http://dx.doi.org/10.1111/1440-1630.12003.

Bouck, E. C. (2013). "High stakes? Considering students with mild intellectual disability in accountability systems." *Education and Training in Autism and Developmental Disabilities, 48*(3), 320–31. Retrieved from https://eric.ed.gov/?id=EJ1016441.

Boushey, A. (2001). "The grief cycle—One parent's trip around." *Focus on Autism and Other Developmental Disabilities, 16*(1), 27–30. http://dx.doi.org/10.1177/108835760101600107.

Boyd, T. K., Hart Barnett, J. E., and More, C. M. (2015). "Evaluating iPad technology for enhancing communication skills of children with autism spectrum disorders." *Intervention in School and Clinic, 51*(1), 19–27. http://dx.doi.org/10.1177/1053451215577476.

Brookman-Frazee, L. I., Drahota, A, and Stadnick, N. (2012). "Training community mental health therapists to deliver a package of evidence-based practice strategies for school-age children with autism spectrum disorder: A pilot study." *Journal of Autism and Developmental Disorders, 42*(8), 1651–61. http://dx.doi.org/10.1007/s10803-011-1406-7.

Brookman-Frazee, L. I., Taylor, R., and Garland, A. F. (2010). "Characterizing community-based mental health services for children with autism spectrum disorders and disruptive behavior problems." *Journal of Autism and Developmental Disorders, 40*(10), 1188–1201. http://dx.doi.org/10.1007/s10803-010-0976-0.

Bryson, S. A., Corrigan, S. K., McDonald, T. P., and Holmes, C. (2008). "Characteristics of children with autism spectrum disorders who received services through community mental health centers." *Autism, 12*(1), 65–82. http://dx.doi.org/10.1177/1362361307085214.

Burak, A., and Parker, L. (2017). *Power Play: How Video Games Can Save the World.* New York: St. Martin's Press.

Cameron, H., and Muskett, T. (2014). "Recognising autism spectrum disorders in primary care: Perspectives of speech and language therapists." *Child Care in Practice, 20*(3), 313–28. http://dx.doi.org/10.1080/13575279.2014.905453.

Cappadocia, M. C., Weiss, J. A., and Pepler, D. (2012). "Bullying experiences among children and youth with autism spectrum disorders." *Journal of Autism and Developmental Disorders, 42*(2), 266–77. http://dx.doi.org/10.1007/s10803-011-1241-x.

Carnahan, C., Williamson, P., and Christman, J. (2011). "Linking cognition and literacy in students with autism spectrum disorder." *TEACHING Exceptional Children, 43*(6), 54–62. http://dx.doi.org/10.1177/004005991104300606.

Case-Smith, J., Weaver, L. L., and Fristad, M. A. (2015). "A systematic review of sensory processing interventions for children with autism spectrum disorders." *Autism, 19*(2), 133–48. http://dx.doi.org/10.1177/1362361313517762.

CAST. (2018). "About universal design for learning." Retrieved from http://www.cast.org/our-work/about-udl.html#.WoBriOjwZPY.

Celli, L. M., and Young, N. D. (2014). *Learning Style Perspectives: Impact in the Classroom* (3rd ed.). Madison, WI: Atwood Publishers.

Centers for Disease Control and Prevention. (2018a). "Facts about ASD." Retrieved from https://www.cdc.gov/ncbddd/autism/facts.html.

Centers for Disease Control and Prevention (2018b). "Autism spectrum disorders: Data and statistics." Retrieved from https://www.cdc.gov/ncbddd/autism/data.html.

Centers for Disease Control and Prevention. (2018c). "Key findings: Trends in the prevalence of developmental disabilities in U.S. children, 1997–2008." Retrieved from https://www.cdc.gov/ncbddd/developmentaldisabilities/features/birthdefects-dd-keyfindings.html.

Centers for Disease Control and Prevention. (2018d). "Autism and Developmental Disabilities Monitoring (ADDM) Network." Retrieved from https://www.cdc.gov/ncbddd/autism/Addm.html.

Centers for Disease Control and Prevention. (2018e). "Centers for Autism and Developmental Disabilities Research and Epidemiology (CADDRE)." Retrieved from https://www.cdc.Gov/ncbddd/autism/caddre.html.

Centers for Disease Control and Prevention. (2018f). "Community report on autism 2018." Retrieved from https://www.cdc.gov/ncbddd/autism/addm-community-report/documents/addm-Community-report-2018-h.pdf.

Centers for Disease Control and Prevention. (2018g). "Study to Explore Early Development (SEED)." Retrieved from https://www.cdc.gov/ncbddd/autism/seed.html.

Chen, P. Y., and Schwartz, I. S. (2012). "Bullying and victimization experiences of students with autism spectrum disorders in elementary schools." *Focus on Autism and Other Developmental Disabilities, 27*(4), 200–12. http://dx.doi.org/10.1177/1088357612459556.

Chiang, H. M., Cheung, Y. K., Hickson, L., Xiang, R., and Tsai, L. Y. (2012). "Predictive factors of participation in postsecondary education for high school leavers with autism." *Journal of Autism and Developmental Disorders, 42*(5), 685–96. http://dx.doi.org/10.1007/s10803-011-1297-7.

Committee for Children. (2018). "Second Step social skills program." Retrieved from https://www.secondstep.org.

Commonwealth of Massachusetts. (2018). "Autism Commission." Retrieved from https://www.mass.gov/orgs/autism-Commission.

Connor, D. J. (2012). "Helping students with disabilities transition to college: 21 tips for students with LD and/or ADD/ADHD." *TEACHING Exceptional Children, 44*(5), 16–25. https://dx.doi.org/10.1177/004005991204400502.

Conrad, A. (2015). *Autism: From denial to acceptance.* Retrieved from https://www.autismspeaks.org/blog/2015/02/19/autism-denial-acceptance.

Conversation, The. (2018). "Supporting students with autism in the classroom: What teachers need to know." Retrieved from http://theconversation.com/supporting-students-with-autism-in-the-classroom-what-teachers-need-to-know-64814.

Cook, B. G., Tankersley, M., Cook, L., and Landrum, T. J. (2008). "Evidence-based practices in special education: Some practical considerations." *Intervention in School and Clinic, 44*(2), 66–75. http://dx.doi.org/10.1177/1053451208321452.

Coriella, C. and Horowitz, S. H. (2014). *The State of Learning Disabilities: Fact, Trends, and Emerging Issues.* New York: National Center for Learning Disabilities. Retrieved from http://www.ncld.org/wp-content/uploads/2014/11/2014-State-of-LD.pdf.

Council for Exceptional Children. (2014). *Standards for Evidence-Based Practices in Special Education.* Arlington, VA: Council for Exceptional Children. Retrieved from http://www.cec.sped.org/~/media/Files/Standards/Evidence%20based%20Practices%20and%20Practice/EBP%20FINAL.pdf.

Cridland, E. K., Jones, S. C., Caputi, P., and Magee, C. A. (2014). "Being a girl in a boys' world: Investigating the experience of girls with autism spectrum disorders during adolescence." *Journal of Autism and Developmental Disorders, 44*(6), 1261–74. http://dx.doi.org/10.1007/s10803-013-1985-6.

Davis, K. M., Boon, R. T., Cihak, D. F., and Fore, C. (2010). "Power cards to improve conversational skills in adolescents with Asperger Syndrome." *Focus on Autism and Other Developmental Disabilities, 25*(1), 12–22. http://dx.doi.org/10.1177/1088357609354299.

Dingfelder, H. E., and Mandell, D. S. (2011). "Bridging the research-to-practice gap in autism intervention: An application of diffusion of innovation theory." *Journal of Autism and Developmental Disorders, 41*(5), 597–609. http://dx.doi.org/10.1007/s10803-010-1081-0.

Dunlap, G., Iovannone, R., Kincaid, D., Wilson, K., Christiansen, K., Stain, P., and English, C. (2010). *Prevent-Teach-Reinforce: The School-Based Model of Individualized Positive Behavior Support.* Baltimore: Brooks Publishing.

Elliot, S. N., and Gresham, F. M. (1991). *SSiS: Social Skills Improvement System: Intervention Guide.* New York, NY: Pearson.

Espelage, D. L. (2017). "Research-informed bullying prevention: Social-emotional learning & school climate improvement approaches." Retrieved from http://www.apa.org/about/apa/archives/bullying-slides.pdf.

Esposito, M., Sloan, J., Tancredi, A., Gerardig, G., Postiglione, P., Fotia, F., Napoli, E., et al. (2017). "Using tablet applications for children with autism to increase their cognitive and social skills." *Journal of Special Education Technology, 32*(4), 199–209. http://dx.doi.org/10.1177/0162643417719751.

Evans Getzel, E. (2014). "Fostering self-determination in higher education: Identifying evidence based practices." *Journal of Postsecondary Education and Disability, 27*(4), 381–86. Retrieved from https://files.eric.ed.gov/fulltext/EJ1060006.pdf.

Family Ties of Massachusetts. (2012). "Parent-to-parent program." Retrieved from http://massfamilyties.org/p2p/p2p.php.

Fenske, E. C., Krantz, P. J., and McClannahan, L. E. (2001). "Incidental teaching: A not-discrete-trial training procedure." In C. Maurice, G. Greem, and R. Fox, eds. *Making a Difference: Behavioral Intervention for Autism,* 75–82. Austin: Pro-Ed.

Finn, L., Ramaswamy, R., Dukes, C., and Scott, J. (2015). "Using WatchMinder to increase the on-task behavior of students with autism spectrum disorder." *Journal of Autism and Developmental Disorders, 45*(5), 1408–18. http://dx.doi.org/10.1007/s10803-014-2300-x.

Fisher, M. H., and Taylor, J. L. (2016). "Let's talk about it: Peer victimization experiences as reported by adolescents with autism spectrum disorder." *Autism, 20*(4), 402–11. http://dx.doi.org/10.1177/1362361315585948.

Friend, M., and Cook, I. H. (2013). *Interactions: Collaboration Skills for School Professionals* (7th ed.). Boston: Allyn and Bacon.

Garbacz, S. A., McIntyre, L. L., and Santiago, R. T. (2016). "Family involvement and parent-teacher relationships for students with autism spectrum disorders." *School Psychology Quarterly, 31*(4), 478–90. http://dx.doi.org/10.1037/spq0000157.

Garbacz, S. A., Witte, A. L., and Houck, S. N. (2017). "Family engagement foundations: Supporting children and families." In M. D. Weist, S. A. Garbacz, K. L. Lane, and D. Kincaid, eds. *Aligning and Integrating Family Engagement in Positive Behavioral Interventions and Supports (PBIS): Concepts and Strategies for Families and Schools in Key Contexts,* 9–30. Eugene: University of Oregon Press.

Gargiulo, R. M. (2015). *Special Education in Contemporary Society.* Thousand Oaks, CA: SAGE.

Garrison-Wade, D. F. (2012). "Listening to their voices: Factors that inhibit or enhance postsecondary outcomes for students with disabilities." *International Journal of Special Education, 27*(2), 113–25. Retrieved from https://files.eric.ed.gov/fulltext/EJ982866.pdf.

Gothberg, J., Peterson, L., Peak, M., and Sedaghat, J. (2015). "Successful transition of students with disabilities to 21st century college and careers." *TEACHING Exceptional Children, 47*(6), 344–51. http://dx.doi.org/10.1177/0040059915587890.

Graham, S., Harris, K., and Chambers, A. (2016). "Evidence-based practice and writing instruction: A review of reviews." In C. MacAuthur, S. Graham, and J. Fitzgerald, eds. *Handbook of Writing Research,* 211–26. New York: Guilford Press Publications, Inc.

Gray, C. (2015). *The New Social Story Book, Revised and Expanded* (15th ed.). Arlington, TX: Future Horizons.

Green, J. M., Hughes, E. M., and Ryan, J. B. (2011). "The use of assistive technology to improve time management skills of a young adult with an intellectual disability." *Journal of Special Education Technology, 26*(3), 13–20. Retrieved from https://eric.ed.gov/?id=EJ1001789.

Gregg, N. (2007). "Underserved and unprepared: Postsecondary learning disabilities." *Learning Disabilities Research & Practice, 22*(4), 219–28. http://dx.doi.org/10.1111/j.1540-5826.2007.00250.x.

Griffin, M. M., Wendel, K. F., Day, T. L., and McMillian, E. D. (2016). "Developing peer supports for college students with intellectual and developmental disabilities." *Journal of Postsecondary Education and Disability, 29*(3), 263–69. Retrieved from https://eric.ed.gov/?id=EJ1123801.

Grigal, M., Hart, D., and Weir, C. (2013). "Postsecondary education for people with intellectual disability: Current issues and critical challenges." *Inclusion, 1*(1), 50–63. http://dx.doi.org/10.1352/2326-6988-1.1.050.

References

Hadley, W. M. (2011). "College students with disabilities: A student development perspective." *New Directions for Higher Education*, (154), 77–81. Retrieved from https://eric.ed.gov/?id=EJ931816.

Haley, M., Hammond, H., Ingalls, L., and Marin, M. R. (2013). "Parental reactions to the special education individual education program process: Looking through the lens of grief." *Improving Schools*, 16(3), 232–43. http://dx.doi.org/10.1177/1365480213505180.

Hamblet, E. (2014). "Nine strategies to improve college transition planning for students with disabilities." *TEACHING Exceptional Children*, 46(3), 53–59. http://dx.doi.org/10.1177/004005991404600306.

Harris, R., Butler, R., Hodgdon, L., and Griffin, S. (2013). *Teach Me with Pictures: 40 Fun Picture Scripts to Develop Play and Communication Skills in Children on the Autism Spectrum*. Philadelphia: Jessica Kingsley Publishers.

Hart, B., and Risley, T. R. (1982). *How to Use Incidental Teaching for Elaborate Language*. Lawrence, KS: H7H Enterprises.

Hart Barnett, and J. E., O'shaughnessy, K. (2015). "Enhancing collaboration between occupational therapists and early childhood educators working with children on the autism spectrum." *Early Childhood Education Journal*, 43(6), 467–72. http://dx.doi.org/10.1007/s10643-015-0689-2.

Higginson, R., and Chatfield, M. (2012). "Together we can do it: A professional development project for regular teachers' of children with autism spectrum disorder." *Kairaranga*, 13(2), 29–40. Retrieved from https://eric.ed.gov/?id=EJ994983.

Hong, B. (2015). "Qualitative analysis of the barriers college students with disabilities experience in higher education." *Journal of College Student Development*, 56(3), 209–26. Retrieved from https://eric.ed.gov/?id=EJ1062866.

HopeLab. (2018). "Project summary—Re-Mission: Where it all began." Retrieved from http://www.hopelab.org/projects/re-mission/.

Hughes, C., Kaplan, L., Bernstein, R., Boykin, M., Reilly, C., Brigham, N., Cosgriff, J., et al. (2012). "Increasing social interaction skills of secondary school students with autism and/or intellectual disability: A review of interventions." *Research and Practice for Persons with Severe Disabilities*, 37(4), 288–307. http://dx.doi.org/10.2511/027494813805327214.

IDEA. (2006). "Sec. 300.114 LRE requirements." Retrieved from https://www.gpo.gov/fdsys/pkg/CFR-2012-title34-vol2/pdf/CFR-2012-title34-vol2-sec300-114.pdf.

Institute of Education Sciences: What Works Clearinghouse. (2015). "Select topics to find what works based on the evidence." Retrieved from https://ies.ed.gov/ncee/wwc/FWW.

Interagency Autism Coordinating Committee, U.S. Department of Health and Human Services. (2014). "Strategic plan for autism spectrum Disorder research: 2013 update." Retrieved from https://eric.ed.gov/?id=ED562027.

Jamison, T. R., and Schuttler, J. O. (2017). "Overview and preliminary evidence for a social skills and self-care curriculum for adolescent females with autism: The Girls Night Out model." *Journal of Autism and Developmental Disorders*, 47(1), 110–25. http://dx.doi.org/10.1007/s10803-016-2939-6.

Jennett, H., Harris, S. L., and Delmolino, L. (2008). "Discrete trial instruction vs. and training for teaching children with autism to make requests." *Analysis of Verbal Behaviors*, 24(1), 69–85. http://dx.doi.org/10.1007/BF03393058.

Joshi, G. S., and Bouck, E. C. (2015). "Examining postsecondary educational predictions and participation for students with learning disabilities." *Journal of Learning Disabilities*, 50(1), 3–13. http://dx.doi.org/10.1177/0022219415572894.

Jung, S., and Sainato, D. M. (2013). "Teaching play skills to young children with autism." *Journal of Intellectual and Developmental Disability*, 38(1), 74–90. http://dx.doi.org/10.3109/13668250.2012.732220.

Karren, B. C. (2016). "A test review: Gilliam, J.E. (2014). *Gilliam Autism Rating Scale–Third Edition (GARS-3)*." *Journal of Psychoeducational Assessments*, 35(3), 342–46. http://dx.doi.org/10.1177/0734282916635465.

Kelly, A., and Tincani, M. (2013). "Collaborative training and practice among applied behavior analysts who support individuals with autism spectrum disorder." *Education and Training in*

Autism and Developmental Disabilities, 48(1), 120–31. Retrieved from https://eric.ed.gov/?id=EJ1016468.

Kessler, D. (2018). "The five stages of grief." Retrieved from https://grief.com/the-five-stages-of-grief/.

Klein, A. (2016). "The every student succeeds act: An overview." Retrieved from https://www.edweek.org/ew/issues/every-student-succeeds-act/index.html.

Koegel, L., Matos-Freden, R., Lang, R., and Koegel, R. (2012). "Interventions for children with autism spectrum disorders in inclusive school settings." *Cognitive and Behavioral Practice, 19*(3), 401–12. http://dx.doi.org/10.1016/j.cbpra.2010.11.003.

Kratochwill, T. R., Hitchcock, J., Horner, R. H., Levin, J. R., Odom, S. L., Rindskopf, D., and Shadish, W. R. M. (2013). "Single-case intervention research design standards." *Remedial and Special Education, 34*(1), 26–38. http://dx.doi.org/10.1177/0741932512452794.

Krupnick, M. (2014). "Colleges respond to growing ranks of learning disabled." Retrieved from http://hechingerreport.org/colleges-respond-to-growing-ranks-of-learning-disabled/.

Kuo, N. C. (2016). "Informing instruction of students with autism in public school settings." *Journal of Educational Issues, 2*(2), 31–47. Retrieved from https://eric.ed.gov/?id=EJ1127551.

Larsen, T., and Samdal, O. (2012). "The importance of teachers' feelings of self-efficacy in developing their pupils' social and emotional learning: A Norwegian study of teachers' reactions to the Second Step program." *School Psychology International, 33*(6), 631–45. http://dx.doi.org/10.1177/0143034311412848.

Le Couteur, A., Haden, G., Hammal, D., and McConachie, H. (2008). "Diagnosing autism spectrum disorders in pre-school children using two standardized assessment instruments: The ADI-R and the ADOS." *Journal of Autism and Developmental Disorders, 38*(2), 362–72. http://dx.doi.org/10.1007/s10803-007-0403-3.

Ledford, J. R., King, S., Harbin, E. R., and Zimmerman, K. N. (2018). "Antecedent social skills interventions for individuals with ASD: What works, for whom, and under what conditions?" *Focus on Autism and Other Developmental Disabilities, 33*(1), 3–13. http://dx.doi.org/10.1177/1088357616634024.

Lee, A. M. (2018). "Individuals with Disabilities Act (IDEA): What you need to know." Retrieved from https://www.understood.org/en/school-learning/your-childs-rights/basics-about-childs-rights/individuals-with-disabilities-education-act-idea-what-you-need-to-know.

Lee, I. (2016). "Winning in college: A guide for student with disabilities." Retrieved from http://www.edsmart.org/students-with-disabilities-college-guide/.

Long, S. (2018). "The autism helper: Social skills." Retrieved from http://theautismhelper.com/category/communication-2/social-skills-communication-2/.

Longtin, S. (2014). "Using the college infrastructure to support students on the autism spectrum." *Journal of Postsecondary Education and Disability, 27*(1), 63–72. Retrieved from https://files.eric.ed.gov/fulltext/EJ1029568.pdf.

Luiselli, J. K., Russo, D. C., Christian, W. P., and Wilczynski, S. M. (2008). *Effective Practices for Children with Autism: Educational and Behavior Support Interventions That Work*. New York: Oxford University Press.

Luterman, S. (2017). "Government committee recommends increase in autism research funding." Retrieved from http://nosmag.org/government-committee-recommends-more-funding-for-autism-research/.

Luyster, R., Gotham, K., Guthire, W., Coffing, M., Petrak, R., Pierce, K., Bishop, S., et al. (2009). "The Autism Diagnostic Observation Schedule—Toddler Module: A new module of a standardized diagnostic measure for autism spectrum disorders." *Journal of Autism and Developmental Disorders, 39*(9), 1305–20. http://dx.doi.org/10.1007/s10803-009-0746-z.

Marquis, E., Jung, B., Schormans, A., Lukmanji, S., Wilton, R., and Baptiste, S. (2016). "Developing inclusive educators: Enhancing the accessibility of teaching and learning in higher education." *International Journal for Academic Development, 21*(4), 337–49. http://dx.doi.org/10.1080/1360144X.2016.1181071.

References

Marshak, L., van Wieren, T., Ferrell, D. R., Swiss, L., Dugan, C. (2010). "Exploring barriers to college students: Use of disability services and accommodations." *Journal of Postsecondary Education and Disability, 22*(3), 151–65. Retrieved from https://eric.ed.gov/?id=EJ906688.

Massachusetts Department of Elementary and Secondary Education. (2018). "Accessibility and accommodations manual for the spring 2018 MCAS grades 3-8 tests." Retrieved from http://www.doe.mass.edu/mcas/accessibility/g3-8manual.docx.

Mattila, M. L., Hurtig, T., Haapsamo, H., Jussila, K., Kuusikko-Gauffin, S., Kielinen, M., Sirkka-Liisa, L., et al. (2010). "Comorbid psychiatric disorders associated with Asperger syndrome/high-functioning autism: A community- and clinic-based study." *Journal of Autism and Developmental Disorders, 40*(9), 1080–93. http://dx.doi.org/10.1007/s10803-010-0958-2.

McCall, Z. (2015). "The transition experiences, activities, and support of four college students with disabilities." *Career Development and Transition for Exceptional Individuals, 38*(3), 162–72. http://dx.doi.org/10.1177/2165143414537679.

McKenney, E. L. W. (2017). "Endrew F. v. Douglas County School District: Implications for teams serving students with autism spectrum disorder." *Communique, 46*(2), 11–12. Retrieved from https://eric.ed.gov/?id=EJ1156714.

Mereoiu, M., Bland, C., Dobbins, N., and Niemeyer, J. A. (2015). "Exploring perspectives on child care with families of children with autism." *Early Childhood Research and Practice, 17*(1), 1–13. Retrieved from http://ecrp.uiuc.edu/v17n1/mereoiu.html.

Michigan Autism Program. (2018). "Michigan Autism Council." Retrieved from https://www.michigan.gov/autism/0,4848,7-294-63678---,00.html.

Miller, K., DiSandro, R., Harrington, L., and Johnson, J. (2016). "Inclusive higher education is reaping benefits for individuals with intellectual disabilities." Retrieved from https://thinkcollege.net/resource/student-outcomes/inclusive-higher-education-reaping-benefits-individuals-intellectual.

Miranda, A., Tarraga, R., Fernandez, M. I., Colomer, C., and Pastor, G. (2015). "Parenting stress in families of children with autism spectrum disorder and ADHD." *Exceptional Children, 82*(1), 81–95. http://dx.doi.org/10.1177/0014402915585479.

Model Me Kids. (2017). "Videos for modeling social skills." Retrieved from http://www.modelmekids.com/index.html.

Morrier, M. J., Hess, K. L., and Heflin, L. J. (2011). "Teacher training for implementation of teaching strategies for students with autism spectrum disorders." *Teacher Education and Special Education, 34*(2), 119–32. http://dx.doi.org/10.1177/0888406610376660.

Murphy, A. N., Radley, K. C., and Helbig, K. A. (2018). "Use of superheroes social skills with middle school-age students with autism spectrum disorder." *Psychology in the Schools, 55*(3), 323–35. http://dx.doi.org.ezai.ez.cwmars.org:3200/10.1002/pits.22104.

Myles, B. S., Trautman, M., and Schelvan, R. (2013). *The Hidden Curriculum for Understanding Unstated Rules in Social Situations for Adolescents and Young Adults* (2nd ed.). Shawnee, KS: AAPC Publishing.

National Autism Association. (2018). "Impact Report 2017." Retrieved from http://nationalautismassociation.org/wp-content/uploads/2018/03/NAA-2017-Impact-Report.pdf.

National Autism Resources. (2018). "The Picture Exchange Communication System (PECS)." Retrieved from https://www.nationalautismresources.com/the-picture-exchange-communication-system-pecs/.

National Autistic Society, The. (2017). "Self-care skills." Retrieved from http://www.autism.org.uk/about/health/self-care.

National Center for Education Statistics. (2016). "Fast facts: Students with disabilities." Retrieved from https://nces.ed.gov/fastfacts/display.asp?id=64.

National Center on Universal Design for Learning. (2014). "What is UDL?" Retrieved from http://www.udlcenter.org/aboutudl/whatisudl.

National Disability Institute. (2018). "ABLE Act." Retrieved from https://www.realeconomicimpact.org/public-policy/able-act.

National Institute of Mental Health. (2018). "Office of Autism Research Coordination." Retrieved from https://www.nimh.nih.gov/about/organization/od/office-of-autism-research-coordination-oarc.shtml.

Neely, J., Amatea, E. S., Echevarria-Doan, S., and Tannen, T. (2012). "Working with families living with autism: Potential contributions of marriage and family therapists." *Journal of Marital and Family Therapy, 38*(S1), 211–26. http://dx.doi.org/10.1111/j.1752-0606.2011.00265.x.

Newman, L., Madaus, J., and Javitz, H. (2016). "Effect of transition planning on post-secondary support receipt by students with disabilities." *Exceptional Children, 82*(4), 497–514. http://dx.doi.org/10.1177/0014402915615884.

Nichols, S., Moravcik, G. M., and Tetenbaum, S. P. (2009). *Girls Growing Up on the Autism Spectrum: What Parents and Professionals Should Know about the Pre-Teen and Teenage Years.* Philadelphia: Jessica Kingsley Publishers.

Nicolaidis, C., Kripki, C. C., and Raymaker, D. (2014). "Primary care for adults on the autism spectrum." *Medical Clinics of North America, 98*(5), 1169–91. http://dx.doi.org/10.1016/j.mcna.2014.06.011.

Organization for Autism Research. (2012). "Life journey through autism: Navigating the special education system." Retrieved from https://eric.ed.gov/?id=ED542647.

Ostmeyer, K, and Scarpa, A. (2012). "Examining school-based social skills program needs and barriers for students with high-functioning autism spectrum disorders using participatory action research." *Psychology in the Schools, 49*(10), 932–41. http://dx.doi.org/10.1002/Pits.21646.

Padden, L., and Ellis, C. (2015). "Disability awareness and university staff training in Ireland (practice brief)." *Journal of Postsecondary Education and Disability, 28*(4), 433–45. Retrieved from https://files.eric.ed.gov/fulltext/EJ1093559.pdf.

Pearson Clinical (2017). "Autism diagnostic interview–Revised (ADI-R)." Retrieved from https://www.pearsonclinical.com.au/products/view/290.

Phillips, N., and Beavan, L. (2012). *Teaching Play to Children with Autism: Practical Interventions using Identiplay.* Thousand Oaks, CA: SAGE.

Picard, D. (2015). "Teaching students with disabilities." Retrieved from https://cft.vanderbilt.edu/guides-sub-pages/disabilities/.

Pierce, D. (2014). "How colleges can better serve students with learning disabilities." Retrieved from https://campustechnology.com/articles/2014/12/18/how-colleges-can-better-serve-students-with-learning-disabilities.aspx.

Pinder-Amaker, S. (2014). "Identifying the unmet needs of college students on the autism spectrum." *Harvard Review of Psychiatry, 22*(2), 125–37. Retrieved from https://www.ncbi.nlm.nih.gov/pubmed/24614767.

Plexousakis, S., Georgiadi, M., and Kourkoutas, E. (2011). "Asperger syndrome and sexuality: Intervention issues in a case of an adolescent with Asperger syndrome in a context of a special educational setting." *Procedia Social and Behavioral Sciences, 15,* 490–95. http://dx.doi.org/10.1016/j.sbspro.2011.03.128.

Positive Behavioral Interventions and Supports. (2018). "Positive behavioral interventions and supports: OSEP Technical Assistance Center." Retrieved from https://www.pbis.org.

Prater, M. A., Redman, A. S., Anderson, D., and Gibb, G. S. (2014). "Teaching adolescent students with learning disabilities to self-advocate for accommodations." *Intervention in School and Clinic, 49*(5), 298–305. http://dx.doi.org/10.1177/1053451213513958.

Radley, K. C., McHugh, M. B., Taber, T., Battaglia, A. A., and Ford, W. B. (2017). "School-based social skills training for children with autism spectrum disorder." *Focus on Autism and Other Developmental Disabilities, 32*(4), 256–68. http://dx.doi.org/10.1177/1088357615583470.

Ramisch, J. (2012). "Marriage and family therapists working with couples who have children with autism." *Journal of Marital and Family Therapy, 38*(2), 305–16. http://dx.doi.org/10.1111/j.1752-0606.2010.00210.x.

Reichow, B. (2012). "Overview of meta-analyses on early intensive behavioral intervention for young children with autism spectrum disorders." *Journal of Autism and Developmental Disorders, 42*(4), 512–20. http://dx.doi.org/10.1007/s10803-011-1218-9.

Ruble, L. A., McGrew, J. H., Dalrymple, N., and Jung, L. A. (2010). "Examining the quality of IEPs for young children with autism." *Journal of Autism and Developmental Disorders, 40*(12), 1459–70. http://dx.doi.org/10.1007/s10803-010-1003-1.

Ruble, L. A., and McGrew, J. H. (2013). "Teacher and child predictors of achieving IEP goals of children with autism." *Journal of Autism and Developmental Disorders, 43*(12), 2748–63. http://dx.doi.org/10.1007/s10803-013-1884-x.

Russa, M. B., Matthews, A. L., and Owen-DeSchryver, J. S. (2015). "Expanding supports to improve the lives of families of children with autism spectrum disorder." *Journal of Positive Behavior Interventions, 17*(2), 95–104. http://dx.doi.org/10.1177/1098300714532134.

Schendel, D. E., Diguiseppi, C., Croen, L. A., Fallin, M. D., Reed, P. L., Schieve, L. A., Wiggins, L. D., et al. (2012). "The study to explore early development (SEED): A multisite epidemiologic study of autism by the centers for autism and developmental disabilities research and epidemiology (CADDRE) network." *Journal of Autism and Developmental Disorders, 42*(10), 2121–40. http://dx.doi.org/10.1007/s10803-012-1461-8.

Searing, B. M. J., Graham, F., and Grainger, R. (2015). "Support needs of families living with children with autism spectrum disorder." *Journal of Autism and Developmental Disorders, 45*(11), 3693–3702. http://dx.doi.org/10.1007/s10803-015-2516-4.

Shane, H. C., Laubscher, E. H., Schlosser, R. W., Flynn, S., Sorce, J. F., and Abramson, J. (2012). "Applying technology to visually support language and communication in individuals with autism spectrum disorders." *Journal of Autism and Developmental Disorders, 42*(6), 1228–35. http://dx.doi.org/10.1007/s10803-011-1304-z.

Shattuck, P. T., Narendorf, S. C., Cooper, B., Sterzing, P. R., Wagner, M., and Taylor, J. L. (2012). "Postsecondary education and employment among youth with an autism spectrum disorder." *Pediatrics, 129*(6), 1042–49. http://dx.doi.org/10.1542/peds.2011-2864.

Shek, D. T. L., and Wong, K. K. (2011). "Do adolescent developmental issues disappear overnight? Reflections about holistic development in university students." *Scientific World Journal, 11*, 353–61. http://dx.doi.org/10.1100/tsw.2011.5.

Silva, L. M. T., and Schalock, M. (2012). "Autism parenting stress index: Initial psychometric evidence." *Journal of Autism and Developmental Disorders, 42*(4), 566–74. http://dx.doi.org/10.1007/s10803-011-1274-1.

Skinner, M. E. (1998) "Promoting self-advocacy among college students with learning disabilities." *Intervention in School and Clinic, 33*(5), 278–83. http://dx.doi.org/10.1177/105345129803300504.

Smith, D. L., and Gillon, G. T. (2004). "Autism spectrum disorder: Caseload characteristics, and interventions implemented by speech-language therapists." *Kairaranga, 5*(2), 46–54. Retrieved from https://eric.ed.gov/?id=EJ914559.

Smith, T. (2012). "Evolution of research on interventions for individuals with autism spectrum disorder: Implications for behavior analysts." *The Behavior Analyst, 35*(1), 101–13. http://dx.doi.org/10.1007/BF03392269.

Social Thinking. (2018). "WeThinkers." Retrieved from https://www.socialthinking.com/Products/WeThinkersVolume1DeluxePackage.

Social Welfare History Project. (2016). "Elementary and Secondary Education Act of 1965." Retrieved from https://socialwelfare.library.vcu.edu/programs/education/elementary-and-secondary-education-act-of-1965/.

Special Learning. (2018). "Pervasive development disorder–not otherwise specified." Retrieved from https://www.special-learning.com/article/Pervasive_Developmental_Disorder_Not_Otherwise_Specified.

Spencer, S. A. (2011). "Universal design for learning: Assistance for teachers in today's inclusive classrooms." *Interdisciplinary Journal of Teaching and Learning, 1*(1), 10–22. Retrieved from https://eric.ed.gov/?id=EJ1055639.

Stagnitti, K. (2018). "Learn to Play." Retrieved from https://www.learntoplayevents.com/about/.

Stanfield, J. (2018). "How to model and teach the art of self-control in your classroom." Retrieved from https://www.stanfield.com/blog/2018/05/teach-self-control/.

Strayhorn, T. L. (2016). *Student Development Theory in Higher Education: A Social Psychological Approach*. New York: Routledge.

Symbionica. (n.d.). FaceSay™ social skills software games. Retrieved from https://www.facesay.com.

Szidon, K., Ruppar, A., and Smith, L. (2015). "Five steps for developing effective transition plans for high school students with autism spectrum disorder." *TEACHING Exceptional Children, 47*(3), 147–52. http://dx.doi.org/10.1177/0040059914559780.

TeachTown (2018). "TeachTown." Retrieved from https://web.teachtown.com/.

Test, D. W., Smith, L. E., and Carter, E. W. (2014). "Equipping youth with autism spectrum disorders for adulthood: Promoting rigor, relevance, and relationships." *Remedial and Special Education, 35*(2), 80–90. http://dx.doi.org/10.1177/0741932513514857.

Thompson, B. N. (2017). "Helping your child with autism improve social skills." Retrieved from https://www.psychologytoday.com/us/blog/socioemotional-success/201706/helping-your-child-autism-improve-social-skills.

Tint, A., and Weiss, J. A. (2016). "Family wellbeing of individuals with autism spectrum disorder: A scoping review." *Autism, 20*(3), 262–75. http://dx.doi.org/10.1177/1362361315580442.

Toca Boca. (2018). "About Toca Boca." Retrieved from https://www.tocaboca.com/apps/.

University of Miami Health System. (2018). "Family Navigator program." Retrieved from http://pediatrics.med.miami.edu/mailman-center/family-navigator-program.

U.S. Department of Education. (1998). "Auxiliary aids and services for postsecondary students with disabilities." Retrieved from www.2ed.gov/about/offices/list/ocr/docs/auxaids.

U.S. Department of Education. (2010). "Thirty-five years of progress in educating children with disabilities through IDEA." Retrieved from http://www2.ed.gov/about/offices/list/osers/idea35/history/idea-35-history.pdf.

U.S. Department of Education. (2011a). "Transition of students with disabilities to postsecondary education: A guide for high school educators." Retrieved from https://www2.ed.gov/print/about/offices/list/ocr/transitionguide.html.

U.S. Department of Education. (2011b). "Students with disabilities preparing for postsecondary education: know your rights and responsibilities." Retrieved from www.2.ed.gov/print/about/offices/list/orc/transition.

U.S. Department of Education. (2016). "Laws and guidance." Retrieved from https://www2.ed.gov/policy/landing.jhtml?src=pn.

U.S. Department of Education, Office of Special Education and Rehabilitative Services, Office of Special Education Programs. (2015). "37th Annual Report to Congress on the Implementation of the Individuals with Disabilities Education Act, 2015." Washington, DC. Retrieved from https://www2.ed.gov/about/reports/annual/osep/2015/parts-b-c/37th-arc-for-idea.pdf.

U.S. Department of Health & Human Services. (2018). "Interagency Autism Coordinating Committee." Retrieved from https://iacc.hhs.gov/about-iacc.overview/.

Vaccaro, A., Daly-Cano, M., and Newman, B. (2015). "A sense of belonging among college students with disabilities: An emergent theoretical model." *Journal of College Student Development, 56*(7), 670–86. Retrieved from http://digitalcommons.uri.edu/cgi/viewcontent.cgi?article=1024&context=hdf_facpubs.

Vanderbilt Peabody College. (2014). "27 Evidence-based practices for students with ASD." Retrieved from https://iris.peabody.vanderbilt.edu/module/asd2/cresource/q2/p06/27-evidence-based-practices-for-students-with-asd/.

Vllasaliu, L., Jensen, K., Hoss, S., Landenberger, M., Menze, M., Schutz, M., Ufniarz, K., et al. (2016). "Diagnostic instruments for autism spectrum disorder (ASD)." http://dx.doi.org/10.1002/14651858.CD012036.

Vohra, R., Madhavan, S., Samamoorthi, U., and St. Peter, C. (2014). "Access to services, quality of care, and family impact for children with autism, other developmental disabilities, and other mental health conditions." *Autism, 18*(7), 815–26. http://dx.doi.org/10.1177/1362361313512902.

Walker, H. M., Holmes, D., Todis, B., and Horton, G. (1987). *The Walker Social Skills Curriculum.* Austin: ProEd.

Walton, K. M. (2016). "Risk factors for behavioral and emotional difficulties in siblings of children with autism spectrum disorder." *American Journal on Intellectual and Developmental Disabilities, 121*(6), 533–49. http://dx.doi.org/10.1352/1944-7558-121.6.533.

Walton, K. M., and Ingersoll, B. (2015). "Psychosocial adjustment and sibling relationships in siblings of children with autism spectrum disorder: Risk and protective factors." *Journal of

Autism and Developmental Disorders, 45(9), 2764–78. http://dx.doi.org/10.1007/s10803-015-2440-7.

WatchMinder (2018). "About WatchMinder." Retrieved from http://www.watchminder.com.

Webber, J., and Scheuermann, B. (2008). *Educating Students with Autism: A Quick Start Manual.* Austin: ProEd.

Weiss, M. (2007). "Social skills: An exclusive target." *Best of The OARacle*, 23–27. Retrieved fromhttps://nces.ed.gov/programs/coe/indicator_cgg.asp.

Westling, D. L., Fox, L., and Carter, E. W. (2014). *Teaching Students with Severe Disabilities* (5th ed.). New York: Pearson.

White, S. W., Keonig, K., and Scahill, L. (2007). "Social skills development in children with autism spectrum disorders: A review of the intervention research." *Journal of Autism and Developmental Disorders, 37*(10), 1858–68. http://dx.doi.org/10.1007/s10803-006-0320-x.

Whyte, E. M., Smyth, J. M., and Scherf, K. S. (2014). "Designing serious game interventions for individuals with autism." *Journal of Autism and Developmental Disorders, 45*(12), 3820–31. http://dx.doi.org/10.1007/s10803-014-2333-1.

Wilkinson, L. A. (2014). *Autism Spectrum Disorder in Children and Adolescents: Evidence-based Assessment and Intervention in Schools.* Washington, DC: American Psychological Association.

Withey, K. L. (2017). "Using apps to develop social skills in children with autism spectrum disorder." *Intervention in School and Clinic, 52*(4), 250–55. http://dx.doi.org/10.1177/1053451216659475.

Wong, C. M., and Koh, H. C. (2016). "Brief report: Investigating the implications of applying the new DSM-5 criteria for diagnosing autism spectrum disorder in a preschool population in Singapore." *Journal of Autism and Developmental Disorders, 46*(9), 3177–82. http://dx.doi.org/10.1007/s10803-016-2841-2.

Woodcock, J., and Olson Beal, H. (2013). "Voices of early college high school graduates in Texas: A narrative study." Retrieved from http://muse.jhu.edu/article/525001.

Wright, P., and Wright, P. (2008). "Wrightslaw game plan: SMART IEPs." Retrieved from http://www.wrightslaw.com/info/iep.goals.plan.htm.

Xin, J. F., and Leonard, D. A. (2014). "Using iPads to teach communication skills of students with autism." *Journal of Autism and Developmental Disorders, 45*(12), 4154–64. http://dx.doi.org/10.1007/s10803-014-2266-8.

Young, N. D., and Bonanno-Sotiropoulos, K. (2018). "Finding a college that fits: Features of campuses that are friendly to students with learning disabilities." In N. D. Young, C. N. Michael, and T. A. Citro, eds. *To Campus with Confidence: Supporting the Successful Transition to College for Students with Learning Disabilities.* Madison, WI: Atwood Press.

Young, N. D., and Jean, E. (2018). "Supporting struggling students on campus: An academic recipe for success." In N. D. Young, C. N. Michael, and T.A. Citro, eds. *Turbulent Times: Confronting Challenges in Emerging Adulthood.* Madison, WI: Atwood Press.

Zablotsky, B., Bradshaw, C. P., Anderson, C. M., and Law, P. (2014). "Risk factors for bullying among children with autism spectrum disorders." *Autism, 18*(4), 419–27. http://dx.doi.org/10.1177/13623613134777920.

Zager, D., Wehmeyer, M. L., and Simpson, R. L. (2012). *Educating Students with Autism Spectrum Disorders: Research-based Principles and Practices.* New York: Routledge.

Zeisler, J. A. (2018). "Overview of college resources for students with disabilities." Retrieved from http://www.bestcolleges.com/resources/disabled-students/.

About the Authors

Dr. Nicholas D. Young has worked in diverse educational roles for more than thirty years, serving as a principal, special education director, graduate professor, graduate program director, graduate dean, and longtime superintendent of schools. He was named the Massachusetts Superintendent of the Year and he completed a distinguished Fulbright Program focused on the Japanese educational system through the collegiate level. Dr. Young is the recipient of numerous other honors and recognitions including the General Douglas MacArthur Award for distinguished civilian and military leadership and the Vice Admiral John T. Hayward Award for exemplary scholarship. He holds several graduate degrees including a PhD in educational administration and an EdD in educational psychology.

Dr. Young has served in the U.S. Army and U.S. Army Reserves combined for over thirty-four years; he graduated with distinction from the U.S. Air War College, the U.S. Army War College, and the U.S. Navy War College. After completing a series of senior leadership assignments in the U.S. Army Reserves as the commanding officer of the 287th Medical Company (DS), the 405th Area Support Company (DS), the 405th Combat Support Hospital, and the 399th Combat Support Hospital, he transitioned to his current military position as a faculty instructor at the U.S. Army War College in Carlisle, Pennsylvania. He currently holds the rank of colonel.

Dr. Young is also a regular presenter at state, national, and international conferences; he has written many books, book chapters, and/or articles on various topics in education, counseling, and psychology. Some of his most recent books include *Securing the Schoolyard: Protocols that Promote Safety and Positive Student Behaviors* (in press); *Sounding the Alarm in the Schoolhouse: Safety, Security and Student Well-Being* (in press); *The Soul of the Schoolhouse: Cultivating Student Engagement* (2019); *From Cradle to*

Classroom: A Guide to Special Education for Young Children (2019); *Captivating Classrooms: Educational Strategies to Enhance Student Engagement* (2019); *Potency of the Principalship: Action-Oriented Leadership at the Heart of School Improvement* (2018); *Soothing the Soul: Pursuing a Life of Abundance through a Practice of Gratitude* (2018); *Dog Tags to Diploma: Understanding and Addressing the Educational Needs of Veterans, Servicemembers, and Their Families* (2018); *Turbulent Times: Confronting Challenges in Emerging Adulthood* (2018); *Guardians of the Next Generation: Igniting the Passion for High-Quality Teaching* (2018); *Achieving Results: Maximizing Success in the Schoolhouse* (2018); *From Head to Heart: High Quality Teaching Practices in the Spotlight* (2018); *Stars in the Schoolhouse: Teaching Practices and Approaches that Make a Difference* (2018); *Making the Grade: Promoting Positive Outcomes for Students with Learning Disabilities* (2018); *Paving the Pathway for Educational Success: Effective Classroom Strategies for Students with Learning Disabilities* (2018); *Wrestling with Writing: Instructional Strategies for Struggling Students* (2018); *From Floundering to Fluent: Reaching and Teaching Struggling Readers* (2018); *Emotions and Education: Promoting Positive Mental Health in Students with Learning Disabilities* (2018); *From Lecture Hall to Laptop: Opportunities, Challenges, and the Continuing Evolution of Virtual Learning in Higher Education* (2017); *The Power of the Professoriate: Demands, Challenges, and Opportunities in 21st Century Higher Education* (2017); *To Campus with Confidence: Supporting the Successful Transition to College for Students with Learning Disabilities* (2017); *Educational Entrepreneurship: Promoting Public-Private Partnerships for the 21st Century* (2015); *Beyond the Bedtime Story: Promoting Reading Development during the Middle School Years* (2015); *Betwixt and Between: Understanding and Meeting the Social and Emotional Developmental Needs of Students during the Middle School Transition Years* (2014); *Learning Style Perspectives: Impact in the Classroom* (3rd ed., 2014); *Collapsing Educational Boundaries from Preschool to PhD: Building Bridges Across the Educational Spectrum* (2013); *Transforming Special Education Practices: A Primer for School Administrators and Policy Makers* (2012); and *Powerful Partners in Student Success: Schools, Families and Communities* (2012). He also coauthored several children's books including the popular series *I am Full of Possibilities*. Dr. Young may be contacted directly at nyoung1191@aol.com.

Dr. Kristen Bonanno-Sotiropoulos has worked in education at various levels for more than a dozen years. Her professional career within K–12 public education included roles as a special education teacher and special education administrator at the elementary and middle school levels. After her tenure in K–12, she transitioned to higher education to teach undergraduate and graduate courses as an assistant professor of special education at Springfield College located in Springfield, Massachusetts, and then moved to assistant professor, director of special education programs at Bay Path University located in Longmeadow, Massachusetts. Dr. Bonanno-Sotiropoulos received her bachelor of science in liberal studies and elementary education with academic distinction as well as a master of science in moderate disabilities from Bay Path University. She recently completed her EdD in educational leadership and supervision at American International College located in Springfield, Massachusetts, where she focuses on her research on evidenced-based special education practices.

Dr. Bonanno-Sotiropoulos's current research interests include, among other areas, effective instructional programs and practices to assist learning-disabled students with meeting rigorous academic expectations at all academic levels from preschool to college; she is a regular presenter at regional and national conferences. Dr. Bonanno-Sotiropoulos has coauthored a series of book chapters related to the unique needs of struggling readers in addition to how higher education institutions can assist special needs students with making a successful transition to college as well as the following coauthored books: *Guardians of the Next Generation: Igniting the Passion for High-Quality Teaching* (2018); *Wrestling with Writing: Instructional Strategies for Struggling Students* (2018); *Paving the Pathway for Educational Success: Effective Classroom Strategies for Students with Learning Disabilities* (2018); and *Making the Grade: Promoting Positive Outcomes for Students with Learning Disabilities* (2018). She can be reached at kbsotiropoulos@baypath.edu.

Dr. Melissa A. Mumby has worked in various levels of K–12 education for over a decade. She began her career as a high school English and drama teacher, and then transitioned into a role as a special educator, working with both middle and high school students. From there she became a special education coordinator for grades K–5, and eventually the special education director for grades K–12 at a local charter school. She is currently an educational team leader for the Springfield Public Schools, Springfield, Massachusetts. Dr. Mumby holds an undergraduate degree in English literature from the University of Massachusetts, Amherst, as well as an MEd and EdD from American International College, both in education. Her dissertation, "Is there an app for that? Teachers' perceptions of the impact of digital tools on literacy in the secondary classroom," focused on the ways in which technology can increase learning outcomes for struggling learners. She has written book chapters on strategies for helping underperforming students find success in the classroom, and she is a primary author on *Securing the Schoolyard: Protocols that Promote Safety and Positive Student Behaviors* (in press) and *Sounding the Alarm in the Schoolhouse: Safety, Security and*

Student Well-Being (in press). Dr. Mumby can be reached at mumbym@springfieldpublicschools.com.

www.ingramcontent.com/pod-product-compliance
Lightning Source LLC
Chambersburg PA
CBHW020742230426
43665CB00009B/524